Tony Robinson is the author of many books on historical and mythological subjects, including *Tony Robinson's Kings and Queens* and *The Worst Jobs in History*. He has written several television series for children, including *Maid Marian and Her Merry Men*, for which he received a BAFTA and a Royal Television Society Award. He presents Channel 4's archaeology series *Time Team* and played Baldrick in *Blackadder*.

Praise for *The Worst Children's Jobs in History*:

'Tony Robinson has written a book that will amuse and inspire even the most reluctant of historians'
TES

'. . . readers will find its blend of gruesome facts and dark humour irresistible . . . fascinating and horrifying reading'
Scotsman

'Kids will love the all-round ghastliness of this history lesson'
Belfast Telegraph

'Salutary food for thought for today's disenchanted youth'
Bookseller

The Worst Children's Jobs in History

TONY ROBINSON

Illustrated by Mike Phillips

MACMILLAN CHILDREN'S BOOKS

First published 2005 by Macmillan Children's Books

This edition published 2006 by Macmillan Children's Books
a division of Macmillan Publishers Limited
20 New Wharf Road, London N1 9RR
Basingstoke and Oxford
www.panmacmillan.com

Associated companies throughout the world

ISBN-13: 978-0-330-44286-2
ISBN-10: 0-330-44286-4

1 3 5 7 9 8 6 4 2

A CIP catalogue record for this book is available from
the British Library.

Designed by John Fordham
Printed and bound in Great Britain by Bath Press

PHOTOGRAPHIC ACKNOWLEDGEMENTS

Bridgeman Art Library: 64, 74; English Heritage: 75; Getty Images: 91, 100; Heritage Image Partnership: 2, 51, 61, 93;
Mary Evans Picture Library: 15, 36; Museum of London Picture Library: 19, 44; Museum of Rural Life: 25;
Science & Society Picture Library: 59, 98; TopFoto: 50, 89; TUC Collections: 95;
From: Henry Mayhew, *London Labour and the London Poor*, 1861–2: 66.

This book is dedicated to

Jo Foster,

who was far more than

a researcher. Indeed this is

her book as much as mine.

Thanks a lot, mate.

Contents

The Worst Children's Jobs in History

INTRODUCTION

Stop Reading This Book Right Now!

Put it down, walk slowly to the kitchen and open the door of the cupboard under the kitchen sink. Off you go!

Don't touch anything. Just look.

Are you back yet? Did you see lots of plastic bottles with names on them like Mr Muscle, Cif, Domestos and Flash? You did, didn't you? And they all said in big, bold letters that they make jobs like cleaning the cooker, washing the kitchen floor and keeping the lav shining bright quick and easy, didn't they?

1

But why is the writer of a book on the worst children's jobs in history asking you to poke about under the kitchen sink, reading a load of old labels?

Because if you'd been alive in the Middle Ages, you wouldn't have had all these bottles of chemicals to make work easy. The point of this book is that every worst job throughout history would have been ten times harder in those days than it is now.

JOB SCORE
Washerboy at lead mine

❄❄❄

COLD: spend all day soaking wet on a hill in the Pennines

💩

FILTH: at least there's plenty of running water around

💤💤

BOREDOM: long hours of discomfort

🪙

CASH: the song goes 'we're bound down to slavery / for fourpence a day'

TOUGH JOBS

If you think you can handle terrible blisters, freezing cold, aching arms, long hours and not much money, you could try being a washerboy, washing the lead ore that your dad has dug up down a Victorian lead mine. How do you wash ore? First you smash it with a hammer, which means dodging the razor-sharp tiny pieces that fly into the air every time you wallop it. Then you collect up all the pieces with your bare hands and put them into a sieve on the end of a pole. After that comes the chilly part. You pump the sieve up and down in a tub of icy cold water. It's not easy. The end of the pole is higher than you are, so you have to jump to reach it. It is back-breaking work and you won't stop shivering. It might not be too bad in summer, but imagine doing this in the middle of winter.

GOOD JOBS

Not all children's jobs were horrible. Every year on 6 December a boy was chosen to be bishop in charge of all the local churches until Christmas was over. It was supposed to remind people how humble Jesus had been. The boy bishop got to wear fancy clothes and could order all the priests around. He could even declare holidays and tell the priests to hand out sweets to the local children. In the sixteenth century Henry VIII decided to ban the whole thing as the boys who were chosen weren't treating it seriously enough. In fact, they were just having a laugh. I don't blame them. Do you?

JOB SCORE
Boy Bishop

CASH: for a while

FILTH: and you get nice new shiny robes

⭐ ⭐ ⭐

GLAMOUR: a few weeks of star status

DANGER: don't get too carried away, you'll be lowly again come Christmas

For instance, let's suppose you'd wanted to do something simple like wash your pants. Before you even got started, you had to make your own washing powder. You would probably have used a handful of wood ash from the fire, or a mix of water and human wee, then rolled your sleeves up and got down to scrubbing away all those stubborn stains.

And if you think that sounds disgusting, other jobs were even stinkier. To make leather you needed a mixture of chicken poo and dog poo, which were mixed up to make a poo gravy and tipped into huge vats. Then you soaked a load of greasy animal skins in the gravy for about twelve months, hacked off the slippery fat and eventually you got leather.

So how come all these children had the free time to do so many worst jobs? Nowadays you're supposed to spend all day at school. But in the Middle Ages, unless you were pretty rich (and a boy), you weren't ever going to need to speak French or to know where Africa was. It was much more important to help your parents in the fields, or get out and earn some cash. And children have so many uses! You can fit into small spaces, like underneath big clanking machines. You've got small, quick fingers, so you're good at making lace or pins. And you've got more energy than grown-ups, which means you can run around a field for twelve hours a day, chasing birds away.

JOB SCORE
Royal Farter

CASH: as much land as you can fart over

FILTH: could get smelly

DANGER: you're safe as long as you can keep 'em coming

BOREDOM: bit of a one-hit wonder?

SILLY JOBS

In the days when children worked like adults, some jobs allowed grown-ups to mess around like kids. Possibly the most childish job of all time wasn't actually done by a young person. There was a grown man who was paid to fart in front of the king, and he was called the Royal Farter.

In medieval England there was a farter called Baldwin Le Pettour who earned his living not only farting, but whistling and leaping around while he did it. He must have put on a really good show. The king found him so funny he gave him a present of a piece of land for making him laugh so much. Maybe you could try it in front of your head teacher and see what he gives you.

So over the years, kids like you have made themselves useful in all kinds of ways that sound terrible to us now.

Of course, jobs don't have to make you puke to count as worst jobs. Maybe they're tiring – so exhausting that you don't have the energy to chew your dinner when you finally stagger home. They can be scary – if you're afraid of the dark, don't try the mining jobs on pages 97-100, and if being shut in a tight space gives you the willies, definitely don't get apprenticed to a chimney sweep like the climbing boys on pages 19-20.

But who knows – you might really enjoy some of the jobs in this book. If you like climbing, what about a job scrambling up the rigging of a naval ship (page 16)? If you're into horses, you could have a go at being a 'riding child', speeding round a Tudor racetrack – if you're racing for the king, make sure you win, because Henry VIII's not the kind of bloke you want to upset. Or if you spend all your time playing on your Playstation, your nimble fingers could come in handy for picking pockets. And although all this might seem a bit of a laugh to you, for the children who really did these jobs it was a matter of life and death.

So do you fancy having a go at some of the worst jobs in history? If you don't, chuck this book in the dustbin right now, but if you do, let's get started on some top jobs that are colder, dirtier, scarier and stinkier than anything you have ever seen in a horror film.

Still with me? OK, let's turn the page.

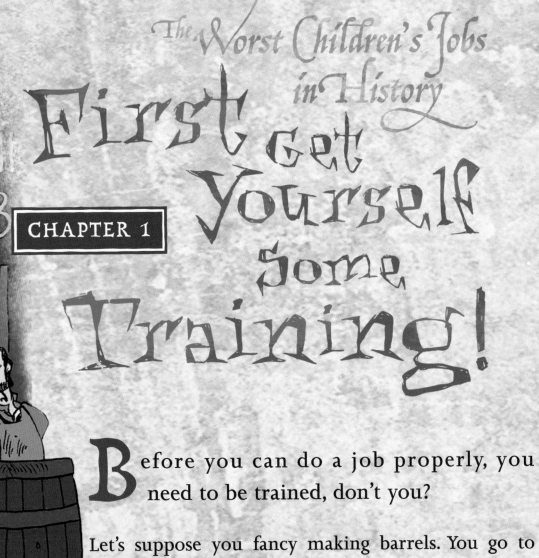

First Get Yourself Some Training!

CHAPTER 1

Before you can do a job properly, you need to be trained, don't you?

Let's suppose you fancy making barrels. You go to a barrel-maker, tell him you want to learn the trade, and what happens next? He covers you with treacle, his mates tip sawdust and flour over you, then they pick you up, stick you in a barrel and roll you round the floor for half an hour.

Is this a ghastly nightmare?

No. If you're going to learn to make barrels, you have to expect this kind of treatment.

In medieval times, if you wanted to learn a skill you became an apprentice, and you almost always had to go through some kind of stupid, humiliating ceremony.

There were hundreds of different trades to choose from. Some were interesting, some of them were useful, but plenty of them were fairly nasty. Lucky children got an apprenticeship with a goldsmith or a merchant. But if your parents didn't have friends in high places, you could end up learning one of the many disgusting, dirty, even death-defying jobs on offer.

Before They Were Famous
DICK WHITTINGTON

Dick Whittington really was Lord Mayor of London. And he did start out as an apprentice to a wealthy merchant. But he wasn't a poor boy from the country who set off with bread and cheese in his knapsack, seeking his fortune in the city where the streets were paved with gold. It's a good story, but in the fourteenth century, if you wanted to be rich, it really helped to have a rich dad. Sure enough, young Dick Whittington was well off from the start.

SIGNING YOUR LIFE AWAY

Before becoming an apprentice, you had to sign a form promising to work for your master for up to ten years. You also had to promise:

*   *not to hang around in pubs*
*   *not to gamble*
*   *not to get married or even engaged*
*   *to be sober, religious, polite and highly respectable.*

If you were apprenticed away from home, you might not see your family for ten years. On the plus side, you'd get your food, lodging, clothes and shoes absolutely free for all that time. The downside was that you wouldn't be paid any actual money.

Pass the Apprentice

As soon as you'd signed your form to become an apprentice, you belonged to your master. You were his property – he could even leave you to someone else in his will. Or if he needed the money, he might sell you.

In 1392 John Bartlet apprenticed his ten-year-old son to a glover, John Parker, for ten years. Soon afterwards, the glover sold the boy to a tailor. And the tailor then sold him to a weaver.

You know that depressing feeling you get when you're the last person picked for the football team? It must have been fifty times worse for little Bartlet Junior.

A BIT OFF THE TOP AND
A BIT OFF MY LEFT LEG, PLEASE

As a **barber's apprentice**, you wouldn't just be sweeping up hair. Medieval barbers doubled as surgeons, so you'd also be mopping up blood. When sick people were thrashing about in agony because they were being cut open, you'd have to hold them still.

And even if you studied hard and became a really good barber–surgeon, you wouldn't be able to save most of your patients. Before anyone discovered the right medicines to kill germs or put people to sleep, many patients who underwent operations died of shock and those who survived the knife often died from infections.

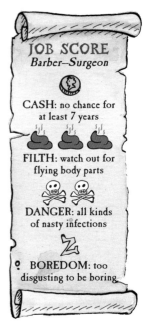

JOB SCORE
Barber–Surgeon

CASH: no chance for at least 7 years

FILTH: watch out for flying body parts

DANGER: all kinds of nasty infections

BOREDOM: too disgusting to be boring

PADDLING IN PEE

You could sign up to be a **fuller's apprentice**, but you'd probably think twice if you knew what was involved. You had to take off your shoes and socks and climb into a barrel full of other people's wee. And not even fresh wee; the best wee was a couple of weeks old. Why would anyone expect you to do a disgusting thing like that? Well, when wool had just been woven, it needed to be tightened up so it wasn't floppy and didn't unravel easily. Treading the cloth in a mixture of ground clay and stale urine tightened it up and gave it a lovely finish. Although maybe it wasn't the greatest way to spend seven years of your life.

THOSE PESKY KIDS

Gangs of teenagers on street corners aren't a new problem. In Elizabethan England, people didn't like the thought of lots of young people hanging out together having fun – particularly bunches of apprentices. So Queen Elizabeth and the Mayor of London made laws saying that apprentices had to stay home after nine o'clock at night and all day on Sundays. And they weren't allowed to play football either.

Mind you, apprentices could create quite a bit of aggravation. In 1595 some of them rioted in Southwark market about the price of fish. Two days later, another group of apprentices was caught throwing stones at the warders of Tower Street.

But they weren't simply told off, or put on probation or even locked up for a few days. They were hanged, their guts were drawn out of their bodies and they were chopped into bits. Well, that certainly taught them a lesson. They wouldn't do that again in a hurry, would they?

HARD AS NAILS

Nail-making workshops in Birmingham took on children as young as seven. While some boys and girls stood at workbenches making the nails, one little kid had the job of working the bellows all day to keep the fire going. Some of the children who did this were so small they had to stand on a box to reach the bellows handle.

And these workshops could really stink. An inspector found one where there was the most disgusting mess sloshing around the floor from an overflowing sewer. The children had to stand on boards so their feet didn't get covered in liquid poo!

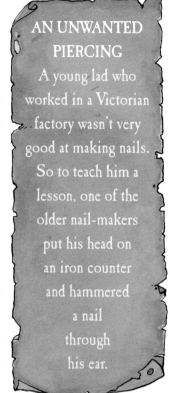

AN UNWANTED PIERCING

A young lad who worked in a Victorian factory wasn't very good at making nails. So to teach him a lesson, one of the older nail-makers put his head on an iron counter and hammered a nail through his ear.

PINS AND NEEDLES

How long could you sit still doing embroidery before you got bored? Five minutes? An hour? How about fifteen hours, with a fifteen-minute break for lunch? That's the amount of time that girls who were apprenticed to **dressmakers** in London had to work.

Being bored was the good part. They also became skinny and pale from spending too much time indoors and not eating enough. Sewing tiny stitches by candlelight ruined their eyesight, and sitting hunched over their work gave them chest pains.

13

But the worst thing must have been the jealousy. The lives of rich Victorian girls were fun, a million miles removed from the drudgery of the young women who slaved away making their beautiful clothes.

Posh girls liked to wear a different outfit each time they went to a swanky ball or party. Their dresses were enormous, and made them look a bit like they'd got an igloo in their pants. Before a really big do, dressmakers had to stay up all night working. And when the rich girls went back to the country at the end of the party season, the dressmakers were out of a job.

JOB SCORE
Dressmaking

DANGER: not fatal but you could go blind

FILTH: not too yucky

BOREDOM: not nearly as fun as parties

HARD SLOG: especially in the party season

ALL AT SEA

FILTH: plenty of
fresh air around

DANGER: if the
cannons don't get you,
the heights might

BOREDOM:
don't forget the
deck-scrubbing

GLAMOUR: for
about the first week

Boys in the eighteenth century thought running away to join **the navy** was really cool. They didn't realize they'd end up haring around a ship in battle, at risk of being killed in any one of a variety of unpleasant ways. For instance, they had to carry barrels of highly explosive gunpowder to the men firing the cannons, so they were likely to be blown to smithereens. If a cannonball hit their ship, they could get speared to death by flying bits of wood. Maybe a

This boy is a 'powder monkey' – he's carrying a keg of gunpowder to the cannons. No wonder he looks like he's concentrating.

cannon would break loose from its moorings and crush them to death or slice off a few limbs as it hurtled round the gundeck. Does a life at sea still sound fun?

Some boys went to sea at the tender age of six. It was thought important that they start young because they needed to be light and agile enough to climb the rigging and work the sails well. This was called 'learning the ropes'. The older boys worked as upper yardmen, right up in the highest sails. This meant they could be working sixty metres above the sea! (That's about the same height as thirteen double-decker buses.)

If this still sounds exciting, there were plenty of boring jobs too. Cleaning out the animals on board was the boys' responsibility, and extremely lucky boys got to spend hours scrubbing down the decks.

Before They Were Famous
CAPTAIN COOK

In 1745 young James Cook was apprenticed to a grocer in Whitby. He found the job so boring it made him determined to go to sea instead. If selling cheese and slicing ham had been more exciting, he might never have discovered Australia!

GONE FISHING

A lot of boys like to catch fish, but this next job definitely isn't the kind of fishing you'd want to do at the weekend. If you were a troublemaker in school back in the 1890s, you might get expelled and be sent to work with the fishing fleet.

Boys of ten and up soon found what put the 'grim' in Grimsby when they became an **apprentice fisherboy** there. They slept on the floor and got up at 5 a.m. to work all day in rain and wind.

16

Boys on trawlers could be away at sea for two weeks at a time, with storms throwing them around the boat. They did heavy work, like hauling huge waterlogged nets on to the deck, and were fed just enough to survive. And as the long weary days went by, the ship was piled higher and higher with slithery fish.

17

Their masters were famous for being mean, and boys often got beaten up just for being seasick. Some of the lads had never even seen the sea before they signed up. They must have been terrified. Lots of them died. You could be put in prison for running away, but at least one third of the boys did. Can you blame them? At least prison wouldn't rock from side to side all the time or stink of herring.

LONG PAST BEDTIME

While he was on holiday in Kent in 1665, Samuel Pepys (famous for writing a diary) got chatting to a local fisherboy. The boy said he hadn't slept in a bed since starting his apprenticeship seven years before, and he still had another two or three years to go!

But the prize for the worst apprenticeship goes to . . .

Sooty the Sweep!

You might think '**climbing boys**' spent their time out in the fresh air, shinning up trees. But you'd be wrong. Actually, it was the name for boy **chimney sweeps** in Victorian Britain. Everyone knows what a horrible job the chimney sweeps had. They were made to crawl through the tightest spaces and brush poisonous soot out of the chimneys.

The younger and smaller a climbing boy was, the smaller the chimney he could get into, so sweeps liked to use kids of six or even

JOB SCORE
Climbing Boy

DANGER: watch out for the fires

FILTH: you'll never be clean

HARD SLOG: tough and painful

CASH: some food if you're lucky

younger. They were supposed to be apprentices, but learned hardly anything at all. Not only that – they were always covered in the filthy, dangerous soot that constantly rained down on them.

So you still fancy being a climbing boy? Before you say yes, look at the picture over the page …

AGE: THE YOUNGER THE BETTER. YOU'LL PROBABLY START WHEN YOU'RE 6 YEARS OLD BUT YOU COULD BE AS YOUNG AS 4. THE GOOD NEWS IS YOU'LL NEVER HAVE TO WORRY ABOUT YOUR WEIGHT. YOUR BOSS WILL MAKE SURE YOU DON'T GET ENOUGH FOOD TO GET FAT.

FACE: IT'LL BE PERMANENTLY FILTHY. YOU GET A BATH AT WHITSUNTIDE (SPRING), GOOSE FAIR (AUTUMN) AND CHRISTMAS. FOR THE REST OF THE YEAR, YOUR FACE IS STAINED BLACK WITH SOOT.

CRY: WHEN YOU'RE WALKING ROUND THE STREETS, YOU HAVE TO SHOUT, 'WEE-EEP!' AS LOUD AS YOU CAN SO PEOPLE WILL COME OUT AND HIRE YOU.

STOOP: YOU MIGHT FIND YOUR BACK STARTS TO BEND AND YOUR SHOULDERS GET HUNCHED. DON'T WORRY. IT HAPPENS TO EVERY CLIMBING BOY. IT'S BECAUSE OF THE HEAVY SACKS OF SOOT YOU HAVE TO CARRY AROUND.

EYES: YOU'LL GET PLENTY OF SOOT IN YOUR EYES. THIS WILL MAKE THEM GO RED AND OOZY.

LUNGS: YOU'LL SOON START TO FIND BREATHING DIFFICULT. THIS IS NORMAL. IT'S JUST WHAT HAPPENS WHEN YOU BREATHE IN SOOT ALL DAY.

KNEES AND ELBOWS: YOU HAVE TO USE THEM TO PRESS AGAINST THE BRICKS, SO THEY'LL GET GRAZED EVERY TIME YOU CLIMB A CHIMNEY. TO HARDEN YOUR SKIN UP, YOUR MASTER MIGHT RUB SALTY WATER INTO THE GRAZES. EXPECT IT TO STING LIKE CRAZY.

CLOTHES: WHEN YOU'RE CLIMBING, YOU'LL PROBABLY WEAR A TUNIC. UNLESS YOU'RE BEING PUNISHED, IN WHICH CASE YOU'LL HAVE TO GO UP NAKED.

FEET: CLEANING CHIMNEYS CAN GIVE YOU SORE FEET. PARTLY BECAUSE OF THE CLIMBING, BUT MORE BECAUSE OF WHAT HAPPENS WHEN YOU STOP CLIMBING. A BIGGER BOY WILL BE SENT UP BEHIND YOU, AND IF YOU SLOW DOWN HE'LL STICK PINS IN YOUR FEET OR TICKLE THEM WITH BURNING STRAW TO GET YOU MOVING.

CANCER: WATCH OUT FOR 'SOOTY WARTS', A KIND OF CANCER THAT CAN KILL YOU. UNFORTUNATELY, IF YOU DO GET IT, THERE'S NO CURE. BUT EVEN IF THERE WAS, YOU WOULDN'T HAVE THE MONEY TO PAY A DOCTOR.

What Happened When

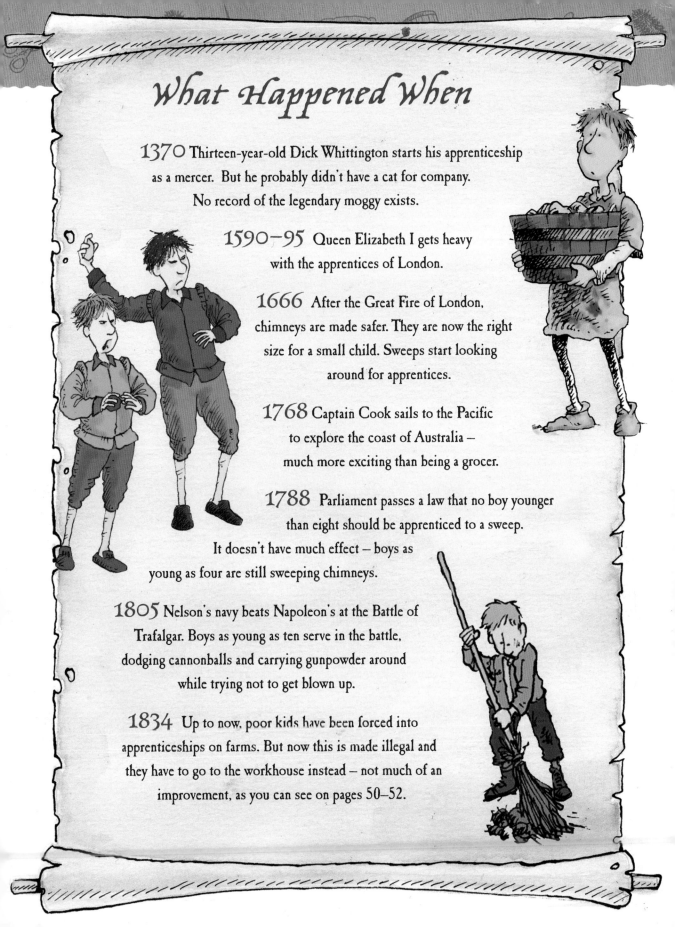

1370 Thirteen-year-old Dick Whittington starts his apprenticeship as a mercer. But he probably didn't have a cat for company. No record of the legendary moggy exists.

1590–95 Queen Elizabeth I gets heavy with the apprentices of London.

1666 After the Great Fire of London, chimneys are made safer. They are now the right size for a small child. Sweeps start looking around for apprentices.

1768 Captain Cook sails to the Pacific to explore the coast of Australia – much more exciting than being a grocer.

1788 Parliament passes a law that no boy younger than eight should be apprenticed to a sweep. It doesn't have much effect – boys as young as four are still sweeping chimneys.

1805 Nelson's navy beats Napoleon's at the Battle of Trafalgar. Boys as young as ten serve in the battle, dodging cannonballs and carrying gunpowder around while trying not to get blown up.

1834 Up to now, poor kids have been forced into apprenticeships on farms. But now this is made illegal and they have to go to the workhouse instead – not much of an improvement, as you can see on pages 50–52.

CHAPTER 2

The Great Outdoors

Ah, the country life! Lying in a haystack, getting sun-tanned, drinking milk from the cow and chomping on bacon butties sliced fresh from the pig.

You must be joking! For most of British history you'd be more likely to have been choked by barley dust, covered in mud, crippled with frostbite or blown up by exploding flour.

If your family was going to have enough to eat, everyone had to keep working. So children did hard, dirty jobs like everyone else, and what's more they did them outdoors, summer and winter. And if you think you'd have enjoyed being out in the fresh air all year, this chapter might just change your mind.

TO AND FRO AND TO AND FRO AND TO AND ...

Every medieval **ploughman** needed a young assistant to shout at the oxen and hit them with a five-metre-long stick called a perch. It was an important job, because otherwise the animals simply stopped moving. But you didn't just wallop them once or twice and then go home for lunch! You had to walk backwards and forwards, poking them with your perch, all day long from dawn to dusk, for miles on end.

And the worst part was, once you'd started working as a ploughman, you were stuck with it. It was such a rubbish job that no one would have done it unless they had to. But the land needed to be turned over, so anyone who knew how to plough wasn't allowed to change their job. You'd be forced to carry on ploughing for the rest of your life.

JOB SCORE
Ploughing

☠

DANGER: OK if you mind the horns

💩

FILTH: like everything else on the farm

HARD SLOG:
walk till you fall asleep, then walk some more

Z Z Z

BOREDOM:
you'd really get to know that field

24

DANGER: VICIOUS COWS

Ploughing wasn't just a long boring walk, holding a stick and staring at an ox's bottom; it could seriously damage your health. In medieval Devon, eight-year-old John Serle of Cheriton Bishop was helping his stepfather plough a field when one of the oxen attacked him with its horns. We know this because a man who wrote about miracles was so shocked that John survived that he thought it must have been an act of God, and so he wrote about it.

THE YOUNG WORZEL GUMMIDGE

JOB SCORE
Bird-scaring

CASH: chicken feed

ZZZ
BOREDOM:
just the birds to talk to

HARD SLOG:
very long hours

FILTH:
relatively undisgusting

Scarecrows are useless, aren't they? Whenever you see one in a field it's got half a dozen crows sitting on its arms and at least one on its hat! You can understand why some farmers preferred live scarecrows. They paid young children to run up and down the fields all day, chasing birds away so they didn't eat the seeds.

Some kids used slingshots. Others, like the little Victorian thug in this picture, were given a clapper made of three bits of wood. Don't worry, he's not trying to squash the birds, just to scare them off. But if you didn't have a slingshot or any wood, you could just shout and flap your arms like a lunatic. George Edwards was sacked from his first ever bird-scaring job at the age of six. He'd got so bored that he fell asleep during his second week at work.

READY-FROZEN TURNIPS

One of the coldest, hardest tasks on a farm was picking turnips for the animals to eat. And it was a job that went mostly to kids.

There's nothing disgusting about turnips themselves, but they had to be picked in the middle of winter. So it'd be freezing in the field, you'd be bending down all day and the frozen ground would be so solid that it would be really hard to pull the turnips up. Plus, your fingers would have turned to icicles and the turnip leaves would have become so frosty they would cut you to ribbons. I love turnips. They're probably my favourite vegetable. But you can see why some people grew up to hate them.

JOB SCORE
Turnip-picking

Z Z
BOREDOM:
pretty tedious

HARD SLOG:
that ground's tough

COLD: watch out
for frostbite

FILTH: the least of
your worries

FARMYARD FILTH

Most jobs in the countryside involved muck, and lots of it! Even something simple like feeding the animals could make you filthy. This was the miserable start of every day for a boy in eighteenth-century Yorkshire who said:

'After breakfast I helped the cowman to feed the stock, staggering along under heavy skips of meal and turnips to some dozen fat bullocks. I was too small to keep out of the muck, and waded through slop and cow-muck until I became absolutely lost. My breeches became so caked in pig-swill, calf-porridge and meal I believe they could have stood upright without me inside them. My hands, by the same process, aided by raw winds, became so swollen and cracked it was purgatory to wash them. And often I didn't.'

THE LITTLEST JOCKEYS

Nowadays jockeys are small adults – but at one time, they were even smaller children. Henry VIII paid 'riding children' to race his horses for him. It must have been pretty dangerous. It's bad enough falling off a horse if you're big, but it's even further to fall if you're tiny.

BEATING THE BOUNDS ... AND THE BOYS

Question: If you were out with your neighbours on a peaceful Sunday walk, why might they have grabbed you by your ankles and dumped you upside-down on your head?

Answer: To make sure you remembered where you were and to make doubly sure you didn't forget it.

Once a year, all the people who lived in your village would go on a long walk all around the parish, checking that no one had stolen their land during the last year by moving the boundaries. When they got to the stone boundary markers, the people in some villages would hit the stones with sticks till they'd worked up a good sweat. In other places, things would get very weird. To drum into the

young boys where the markers were, a variety of methods was used, some violent, some surprising and others downright daft.

At St Cuthberts in 1752 the villagers stopped and beat a boy at each marker.

Scopwick had holes instead of markers, and a boy had to stand on his head in each hole.

Huntingdon also had holes. In 1892 a boy had to stand in every hole while his mates hit him with a spade.

In other villages, boys had their heads whacked against the stones.

Some boys were swung round by their hands and feet and slammed head first into a tree.

To avoid all this violence, couldn't someone have painted the word 'boundary' on a few big signs? Then it wouldn't have mattered whether or not anyone remembered where the stones were!

JOB SCORE
Beating the bounds

BOREDOM: too weird to be dull

DANGER: getting beaten up can be risky

HARD SLOG: more of a day off

CASH: some villages gave you cash or ale to make up for it

Chaff is the part of the grain you don't eat. It's light, so if you hit the grain hard enough the chaff flies off. This is called **threshing**.

In the nineteenth century, machines were invented that could thresh grain more quickly and efficiently than ever before. But they spewed out huge amounts of chaff, which had to be cleared up.

When one of these new threshing machines came round to your farm, all of a sudden there was a brand-new worst job on offer. The men fed the grain in at one end, and a boy stood at the other end where all the chaff was flying out. While he was being showered in sharp, scratchy dust, he had to bag up the chaff as fast as he could. Imagine! It got in your eyes, up your nose, down your neck and up your trousers. It was the tickliest, itchiest job outside a flea circus.

WHERE DID YOU GET THAT HAT?

Straw bonnets were very fashionable in the nineteenth century, and there were armies of young kids to make them. From the age of four, country children sat indoors **plaiting straw**. But in order to keep it supple so they could weave it properly, they had to moisten it with their own spit. I wonder what the rich people would've said if they had known that country kids had gobbed all over their hats.

JOB SCORE
Straw-plaiting

FILTH: at least it's your own spit

DANGER: it's indoor work

HARD SLOG: work or be punished

CASH: not enough to buy your own straw hat

HUNT THE CORN STALK

Scything the corn at harvest time was a man's job. But when the men had been through a field and taken all the corn away for the farmer, children came in with their mums to '**glean**'. They would walk along, searching between the cut-off stalks for any tiny bits of corn that had been missed by the harvesters. It was worth doing, because you could gather enough flour to make bread that would last you through the winter – but only if you worked stupidly long hours. In 1843 Mrs Stone took her three daughters gleaning, but it was hardly a nice family day out. They got up for work at 2 a.m., had to walk seven miles just to get there, and got back home at 7 p.m.!

JOB SCORE
Gleaning

BOREDOM: as tedious as it gets

HARD SLOG: walking for miles, AND bent double

CASH: maybe some corn if you're lucky

GLAMOUR: no excitement to this job

Children were often left to watch sheep. Mostly that wasn't very exciting, although if you were a **shepherd boy** and your flock was in a field of clover, you had to keep an eye out. Sheep love clover, but if they eat too much they get a bad case of wind. If you saw one of your sheep getting fat on the stuff, you had to act quickly. It was risky, but you could save the sheep's life by sticking a small knife in exactly the right spot on its belly. Once you'd done it, you had to stand well back as it slowly deflated like a three-day-old party balloon. And unless you wanted to spend the rest of the day smelling of sheep's farts, you had to remember to stand very well back indeed!

HERE'S A DISGUSTING IDEA

How would you like to be injected with your friend's pus? That's what happened to eight-year-old James Phipps in 1796. He was used as a human guinea pig for Dr Edward Jenner, who was trying out his smallpox vaccine. No one knew for certain if it would work. Dr Jenner took the pus from a sore on a milkmaid who had cowpox and put it straight into James's blood.

Luckily for James, vaccination saved him from the dreaded smallpox, and went on to save millions more lives. But at the time, it must have made little James want to throw up.

DAMSEL IN DISTRESS

After all that hard slogging in the fields, you'd think country children would have been glad of an indoor job. Not the 'damsel' in a nineteenth-century flour mill who risked burning to death. As young as six, she had to work ten hours a day, making sure grain went on to the millstones fast enough. If it didn't, a spark could fly off the empty stones. The air was full of flour dust, which is explosive. So if the girl nodded off for a minute, the whole place could go bang. She also had to watch out to make sure she didn't get caught in the machinery. If she did, she'd be ground to bits along with the flour. Could you have concentrated that hard for ten hours at a time when you were six?

JOB SCORE
Damsel

FILTH: OK if you
don't mind flour

ZZZ
BOREDOM: white,
white and more white

DANGER: mind out
for explosion

HARD SLOG:
pretty long hours

HOPPING MAD

JOB SCORE
Hopping

FILTH: foul huts
to live in

HARD SLOG:
hardly a holiday

CASH:
not quite worth it

GLAMOUR: looked
down on by everyone

You didn't have to live in the countryside to have a worst job in farming. In the 1930s families from the East End of London couldn't afford real holidays. So instead, they went to Kent every summer and spent six weeks picking hops, which were used to make beer. Even the youngest children were put to work as soon as they were big enough to hold a branch.

The hops were spiky, wet and covered in sticky pollen, and they made a right mess of your hands. The writer George Orwell tried it once, and his hands were still scarred a month later. And instead of a nice holiday cottage, you had to sleep crowded together in a corrugated-iron hut on a bed of sticks.

These people look pretty miserable, don't they? It's not my idea of a holiday.

At 7 a.m. there was a bugle call to wake everyone up, and then you had to graft for ten hours in the hop gardens. If you worked really hard, you might make just enough money to pay for some new clothes for your 'back to school' outfit. And you weren't always made to feel welcome – many of the local people thought Londoners were rude, dirty criminals. The East Enders' lives must have been pretty dreadful if they thought this was a holiday!

But the prize for the worst job in the great outdoors has to go to . . .

Being in a Farm Gang!

All farm jobs were tough, but things could get even tougher if you had to work as part of a **farm gang**. From the 1820s, lots of farmers stopped paying men to work for them and saved money by getting gangs of women and children to do the jobs instead. Your gangmaster probably lived in the same village as you, and when a farmer asked him to do something like picking a field of turnips, he'd come round and tell you he had a job for you. The next morning you'd be off to work, with the gangmaster checking up on you in case you slowed down.

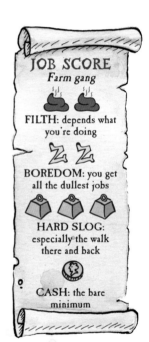

JOB SCORE
Farm gang

FILTH: depends what you're doing

BOREDOM: you get all the dullest jobs

HARD SLOG: especially the walk there and back

CASH: the bare minimum

Kids as young as five were made to walk miles to work in these gangs. Sometimes they'd have to jog all the way, if their gangmaster wanted to make extra money by getting them to work early. They could spend up to fourteen hours at a stretch in a cold field, spreading manure, weeding or, the most pointless job of all, picking up stones from the ground.

No Talking At The Back

Gangmasters were famous for being drunk, mean and uncaring. When one woman from East Anglia was telling people about her childhood, she said she had worked with forty other children between five and eight years old, 'followed all day by an old man carrying a long whip in his hand which he did not forget to use'.

If you were caught talking, you could be pushed face down into a ditch full of water. Or you might get 'gibbeted'. This means that the gangmaster grabbed you by the neck and lifted you off the ground until your face turned black. Even the punishments in schools in those days weren't as bad as that.

Stone-picking involved spending all day bent double with your apron folded up into a big pocket, so you could put the stones in it. If that didn't give you backache, nothing would.

But the stupid thing was that it has since been proved that the crops didn't grow any better in fields without stones than they did in fields that still had lots of stones. What a rotten waste of time!

This boy's been hoeing for so long he's collapsed. I bet the others get told off for slowing down to watch.

What Happened When

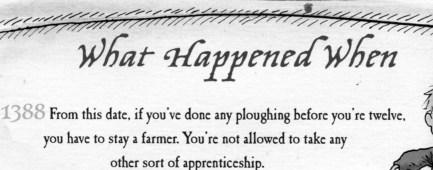

1388 From this date, if you've done any ploughing before you're twelve, you have to stay a farmer. You're not allowed to take any other sort of apprenticeship.

1530 One of Henry VIII's riding boys is paid 10 shillings to run a race (about £160 in today's money). Sounds like he was a good jockey!

1650 Around this time, some farmers experiment with growing clover to improve their fields. And shepherd boys have to start popping their bloated sheep.

1786 The threshing machine is invented. Boys across the country get showered in chaff.

1796 Dr Jenner injects James Phipps with diseased pus — for scientific reasons, of course.

1805 Samuel Wyatt builds himself a farm at Shugborough, with the latest in shiny new farming technology. His flour mill, which needs a six-year-old to run it, still explodes from time to time.

1850 For the first time, more people in Britain live in towns than in the countryside. Which means all the more work for the kids left behind.

1873 From now on, it's illegal for children younger than eight to work on farms. But as always, just because something's illegal, it doesn't mean everyone stops doing it.

The Worst Children's Jobs in History

No Hiding Place

Don't think you could escape from worst jobs simply by crawling back to your nice cosy house and vegging out. Until a hundred or so years ago most houses were damp, cold, stinky and brimful of rotten jobs.

Not only that, but would you fancy sharing your home with a pig? Or how about with a pair of geese, a few chickens, a family of mice, a couple of hundred fleas and a bedful of bedbugs? It doesn't sound great, does it?

But in the Middle Ages you'd have had to. Most families were peasants, and they brought their animals indoors at night so they could keep an eye on them. You can imagine how smelly your house would have been, and the lack of hygiene and air pollution would have been pretty serious too.

There were no bathrooms or inside toilets, and definitely no TV or central heating. A peasant family's house was heated by a smoky fire, and at night it was lit by greasy tallow candles made of animal fat. There was no running water, windows were just little holes in the walls, and the walls themselves were covered in a mixture of mud, straw and horse poo called wattle and daub.

Even worse, you were hardly ever able to get out and about. Until the Victorian age, most people didn't even get to go to school, so you'd have spent virtually your whole time stuck inside your stinking little hovel.

Still, at least you'd have had plenty to keep you occupied. There was loads of hard work to be done around the house, and you were the person who had to do it.

When everyone who was old enough was out working in the fields, the next oldest boy or girl would be left at home to look after the babies. There were so many dangers around the house that this was a tough job. The little mites could toddle into an open fire or wander outside and into a pond. They could even fall into the stinking cesspit at the bottom of the outside loo and never be seen again. To stop babies crawling off and getting into trouble, they were often tied up in cloths like an Egyptian mummy.

But that couldn't save them from all the killer diseases going round. One in five babies died before their first birthday, often from scrofula, which gave you a swollen neck and oozing ulcers, or the bloody flux, a violent attack of diarrhoea that killed you in days.

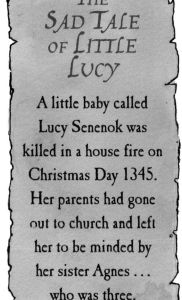

THE SAD TALE OF LITTLE LUCY

A little baby called Lucy Senenok was killed in a house fire on Christmas Day 1345. Her parents had gone out to church and left her to be minded by her sister Agnes ... who was three.

Babysitting nowadays is usually a pretty easy way to earn a bit of money. But 600 years ago, it could be a really terrible job.

GOING TO THE BOG

If you didn't want your toes to freeze off in the icy British winter, you had to build a fire. But you couldn't pop out to the nearest DIY store and pick up a bag of fuel. Maybe you'd go into the woods and collect sticks, but that would take hours and was likely to be pretty boring. If you lived near marshland there was an alternative. You could visit your local bog and **cut peat** instead.

Peat is rotten vegetable matter which looks and feels pretty much like mud. It would have been your job to cut squares of it out of the soggy bog and leave them to dry. Then you had to lug them home so they could be put on the fire. They were cold, heavy and very, very squelchy. Nevertheless this was a million times better than trying to sleep in an unheated house in January.

But it wasn't just household chores that you had to do when you were stuck at home. Your mum and dad, not to mention your brothers and sisters and uncles and aunts, probably brought their work home with them, and you'd be expected to help.

JOB SCORE
Peat cutting

FILTH: messy but not disgusting

BOREDOM: pretty simple

DANGER: not much to fear

HARD SLOG: peat can be heavy

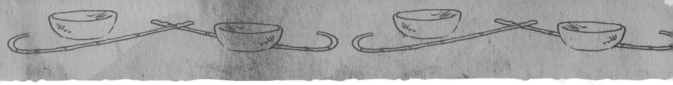

JOB SCORE
Pin-making

FILTH: cleaner
than most

BOREDOM:
numbs your mind
and your fingers

HARD SLOG:
you have to make
thousands of pins

CASH: very low

DULL, BUT NOT POINTLESS

In the days before zips, Velcro and poppers, everyone used pins. People stuck them in their jackets, their dresses, their caps and their aprons to hold the material together, not to mention poking hundreds of them into their fancy ruffs to make sure they stayed frilly. Pins were easy to lose, so people bought loads. In a **pin-maker** family, everyone had to pitch in to make enough. You'd have had to sit round the kitchen table every night pin-making as soon as you were old enough not to stick them in your mouth and swallow them.

There were four easy steps in pin-making:

1) Take some wire.

2) Sharpen one end.

3) Wind more wire round the other end to make the pinhead.

4) Repeat for the rest of your life.

It was so easy, even a four-year-old child could do it . . . which is why they did.

AND HERE ARE 2,000 LITTLE BOXES I MADE EARLIER ...

In Victorian London, match companies liked to save money by getting people to work at home rather than employing them in expensive new factories. Hundreds of women were sent little wooden assembly kits to make into **matchboxes**. But however hard a woman worked, it was impossible to earn enough to feed her children on her own. The whole family would have to work to feed itself.

Each child had its own job. The biggest one glued the boxes, the second biggest made the drawer, the third biggest stuck on the sandpaper and the littlest one slotted the drawer into the box. It was like *Blue Peter*, except that if you didn't make enough boxes, you starved to death.

A mother-and-daughter professional matchbox-making team. They're probably wishing they had another two or three kids to help out.

JOB SCORE
Matchbox-making

Zzz

BOREDOM:
stick the same strip
on day after day

DANGER:
not too hazardous

HARD SLOG: keep
on sticking

CASH: hardly worth
your time

IT WASN'T ALL WORK ...

1. *Question:* Why did children fill a pig's bladder with peas?

Answer: To make a football. For medieval kids the football season started in November, because that's when the pigs were slaughtered.

2. Today many children celebrate Shrove Tuesday by being sick from eating too many pancakes. In the Middle Ages, vicious cockerels were brought into school on Pancake Day. The teachers would let the children off lessons for the day, and they would have a good old-fashioned cockfight, which makes non-uniform days seem pretty tame, doesn't it?

A few children managed to escape these homely jobs for a few hours each day. These were the ones who were lucky enough to go to school. Actually they weren't that lucky. School was yet another place where they were bullied, beaten and overworked.

THE UNKNOWN WHIPPING BOY

If you think your teachers are mean, consider yourself lucky you're not living in the Middle Ages. A good teacher back then was supposed to thump his pupils regularly. You could be whipped by a teacher even if you'd never set foot in his school. Each new teacher in medieval Cambridge was given a hymn book and a birch rod. Then a poor boy from the village was brought in for him to beat, just to prove he was strong enough to be a proper teacher.

THE FAMOUS WHIPPING BOY

The royal **whipping boy** sat next to a prince in lessons. Every time the prince gave a wrong answer, the whipping boy got hit. This may seem ridiculously unfair, but people thought the royals were so special that ordinary people weren't allowed to touch them. Whacking a prince would have been as bad as treason. This was a problem for teachers, because beating their pupils was an important part of their job – so they walloped a substitute instead.

Whipping boys were rich kids who grew up with the prince and became powerful adults. Will Murray, who was Charles I's whipping boy, may have got a sore bottom occasionally, but he ended up with a cushy job at court and the title of Earl of Dysart.

JOB SCORE
Unknown whipping boy

BOREDOM: at least it's over quickly

DANGER: it's bound to hurt

CASH: money for old rope

GLAMOUR: nobody's heard of you

JOB SCORE
Famous
whipping boy

ZZ

BOREDOM: you have
to go to school

DANGER: a good
chance of a sore bum

CASH: you're rich
and getting richer

GLAMOUR: pals
with the king and your
future's rosy

DUH!

CHARITY CASES

In the nineteenth century charity schools were set up for poor
children. But they didn't learn maths or geography. They spent their
days praising God and doing boring jobs like knitting stockings
and making lace.

Going to a **lace-making** school sounds like a bit of a doddle. But
bending over lace pillows gave you a stoop, and the corsets you were
made to wear dug into your chest. Even worse, peering at your

work in poor light ruined your sight. There was no talking, and even in the breaks you'd be kept busy stuffing pillows with straw. You might start at lace-making school as young as five years old, and if you made a mistake, the teacher would push your face down hard on to the lace pillow . . . which had pins sticking out of it.

These lace-makers have been allowed to sit outside – and they still look miserable.

STAY STUPID

Rich people didn't want poor children to learn much at the charity schools. They thought they might get funny ideas and start wanting good jobs or time off.

In 1728 the pastor Isaac Watts said that 'the Children of the Poor should not be generally educated in such a Manner as may raise them above the services of a lower station'.

As far as people like him were concerned, the point of charity schools was to turn out nice, obedient, stupid workers. He also wrote a cheery hymn for children telling them that if they jeered at holy men, God would cut their lips off. Seems he wanted the poor to be scared as well as thick.

PLAYTIME? WHAT PLAYTIME?

One of the best parts of school is playtime. But some Victorian girls didn't get any time off for a break at all. The government thought of something much more useful. The girls were told to spend every break **cleaning** the classrooms. That way, by the time they left school and became servants or mothers, they would be really good at polishing furniture!

POSH SKIVVIES

Even posh kids sometimes got to do worst jobs. As if being sent away from home to a famous boarding school wasn't bad enough, when you got there you would become a '**fag**', a personal slave to an older boy. A sixth-former could order you to make his toast, clean his shoes or smuggle booze into school for him. If you let the fire go out in his room, he burned a mark on your hand.

And there was no point running to tell a teacher. He'd probably just tell you fagging was character building. Never mind – in a few years, you'd have your own fags, and then you could be as mean to them as you liked.

JOB SCORE
Fag

BOREDOM:
too nerve-wracking
to be boring

HARD SLOG: you're
the skivvy to a bully

CASH: not likely

GLAMOUR:
expect to be ignored
and insulted

Before They Were Famous
ROALD DAHL

Over the last couple of centuries, lots of famous men have started their careers as public-school fags. In his book *Boy*, the author Roald Dahl wrote about being made to do lots of stupid, humiliating jobs, like warming up the toilet seat for a sixth-former. Maybe fagging did build character after all: Roald's books wouldn't be nearly so popular if they weren't full of disgusting bits and evil bullies.

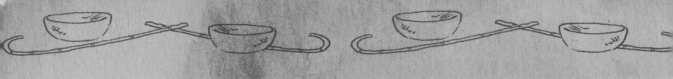

But the prize for the worst place to work has to go to ...

The Workhouse

PLEASE SIR – I WANT TO GET OUT!

JOB SCORE
Workhouse inmate

FILTH: they're horrible places

BOREDOM: it's hardly ever playtime

HARD SLOG: some of the toughest work around

CASH: a bit of gruel if you're lucky

At least all these children had schools or a home to go to. If you were homeless, or your parents couldn't afford to keep you, you might end up in the dreaded **workhouse**, a bit like a cross between a prison and a factory. So great was the fear of these places that some people preferred to starve.

When you went into a workhouse, you'd be split up from your parents, because men, women and children had to live separately there. You'd also get a terrible haircut and an ugly uniform so you looked the same as everyone else – even girls had their hair cut

INTERIOR OF AN ENGLISH WORKHOUSE UNDER THE NEW POOR LAW ACT.

A poster showing how horrible the workhouses were. The people at the front are picking oakum.

short. Overcrowding meant that kids often slept three to a bed. And the beds could just be wooden planks covered with an 8-cm-thick mattress made of straw.

Workhouses were so unhealthy that the merchant and reformer Jonas Hanway reckoned babies in London workhouses were unlikely to live longer than a month. Inmates were crowded together, with not enough to eat but plenty of work to do.

51

The jobs on offer included:

• **sewing sacks** – thick sacking material was very hard to sew, so that by the end of a day you'd end up with bleeding fingers.

• **crushing bones** – this was stopped in 1845 after some inmates were caught eating the rotting meat from the bones they were supposed to be crushing. Imagine how bad the workhouse meals must have been to make this seem a good idea.

• **picking oakum** – you were given a huge pile of old rope, which you had to pull to pieces. Oakum-picking was very fiddly and scraped your fingers raw.

If these jobs sound bad, it's because they were supposed to. The whole idea was that poor people would do any other job at all rather than go into the workhouse.

Before They Were Famous
CHARLIE CHAPLIN

Charlie Chaplin was just seven when he went into Lambeth workhouse. His mum and brother went there too, although the boys were immediately separated from their mother. Later on, Charlie became a rich and famous movie star. But he never forgot what it was like to be poor, and his most famous character in the silent movies he acted in was a little tramp.

What Happened When

1642 Civil War starts in England. Ex-whipping boy Will Murray joins the king's army and is made Earl of Dysart as a reward.

1732 From now on paupers have to go into the workhouse if they want any benefits.

1848 The Public Health Act says that every home should have clean water and a proper toilet. About time too!

1861 A government official decides girls should clean their schoolrooms at breaktime. Seems like an excuse for cutting costs on the cleaning staff.

1880 School attendance is made compulsory for the first time.

1896 Seven-year-old Charlie Chaplin enters the Lambeth workhouse.

1929 Thirteen-year-old Roald Dahl goes to Repton School where he is made to fag for the older boys.

1930 End of workhouses in England and Wales.

1987 Sobbing schoolmasters hang up their canes as beating children is made illegal in state schools. It was still legal in private schools until 1999.

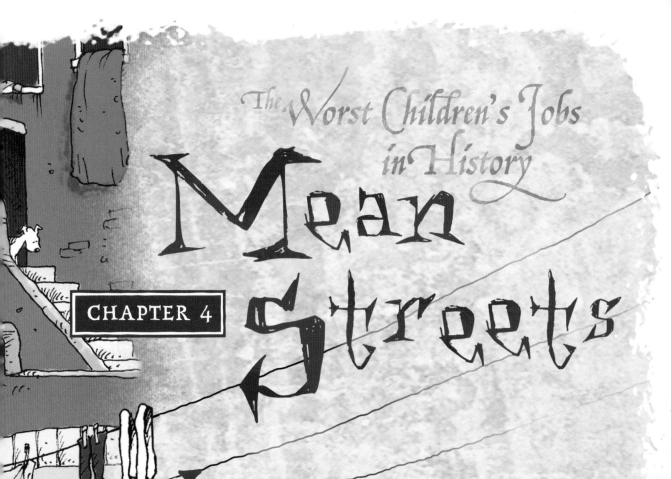

The Worst Children's Jobs in History
Mean Streets

Imagine waking up to find you've got huge black boils all over your body, or that you've turned blue and are vomiting blood.

That's the kind of risk you ran if you worked on the city streets. But there was money to be made there, and for most children who lived in a town and needed to work for a living, the street was the place to be.

But cities were crowded and they stank. Proper sewers hadn't been invented. People used buckets as toilets, and then chucked the contents out of the window into the street below. So it was easy to catch horrible diseases.

Six hundred and fifty years ago you might have died of the Black Death, a disgusting illness in which hard pus-filled lumps appeared in your armpits and groin. It could also make you cough up blood and even see visions. Four days later you would most likely be dead.

One hundred and fifty years ago you could have caught cholera, a revolting disease that caused such bad diarrhoea and vomiting that it killed you. Cholera victims got terrible cramps in their belly and limbs, their raging thirst drove them crazy and their skin turned blue.

Even illnesses like colds and flu could have killed you, particularly if you couldn't afford any medicine or time off work. But if you managed to dodge the host of foul pestilences that lurked in the city gutters, you'd still have had a problem feeding yourself, unless you'd been born rich. And the trouble you could run into earning a few pence in the street could be very big indeed.

Before They Were Famous
CHARLES DICKENS

Twelve-year-old Charles found himself abandoned on the streets when his family was put in debtors' prison for being bankrupt. Luckily, he managed to find a job in a blacking factory, sticking labels on jars (not particularly lucky, but there you go). Later, when he was a famous writer, he didn't forget the poor kids of London and wrote about them to make sure they'd be remembered.

HUMAN HEADLIGHTS

In the eighteenth century, before modern street lights were invented, you could make a few coins as a **link-boy**. First, you needed a link, which was a stick with cotton and wax on the end. Next you lit it. Then you hung around in a dark, dangerous part of town, waiting to see if some smartly dressed gent wanted help getting home.

Yes, you were offering yourself up as a human headlight. You'd get very tired because you had to work so late, and you could easily burn your hands. But the big problem was that walking through the gloomy streets with a rich person while carrying a big flaming torch was like holding a huge illuminated arrow with the words 'Robbers, please mug us!' on it in flashing lights.

Another problem was that the flash bloke who'd employed you might be drunk and puke all over you, or beat you up, or even worse. Link-boys were prepared to take these risks, but what they were really scared of was the moon. On a bright night, no one needed a link-boy, so they couldn't earn any money to buy food. It's little wonder they were also known as moon-cursers.

This is exactly the kind of bloke you want to find. He's rich, he's sozzled, and probably a bit dim. He'll definitely need help finding his way home.

57

THE BLEEDING TOOTH FAIRY

If your job as a link-boy wasn't earning you enough to eat, you might have to turn to this really painful job. Once you were old enough to have grown your second teeth you could make money out of them. People in the eighteenth century were crazy for sugar. They loved it so much they even started the slave trade to get more of the stuff. But sugar rots your teeth, so many of the rich people in the city who could afford to shovel down lots of sugary food ended up with a mouthful of black stumps. So now they needed false teeth. There were lots of ways of making them; some were made out of metal, others of ivory. But one way was to pull the rotting stump from an adult's mouth, and stuff a freshly plucked child's tooth into the bleeding hole.

JOB SCORE
Tooth donor

FILTH:
very unhygienic

DANGER:
pray your tooth doesn't get infected

HARD SLOG:
just open your mouth

CASH: good but not a steady wage

The Edinburgh dentist John Hunter liked to have a row of **tooth donors** waiting so that he could pull a tooth from one child, try it in his patient's mouth, and if it didn't fit he could just keep on going down the line, till he found one that did. Imagine the pools of blood and tears. Modern painkillers weren't invented for another fifty years.

DON'T TRUST THIS WOMAN

In 1775 a female French dentist named Madame de St-Raymond came to York and put up an advert, saying she could 'transplant teeth from the front of the jaws of poor lads into the heads of any Lady or Gentleman without putting both patients to any anguish'. Remember, this was in the days before you could have your mouth numbed with an injection or gas when you were having a tooth taken out.

This picture shows a famous dentist transplanting a tooth from a chimney sweep to a rich woman in 1787. The children leaving the room are nursing their aching gums and looking at the money they had been paid.

HUMAN TEXTING

The Victorians had an alternative to sending a text: they sent a small child instead. **Messenger boys** stood on little boxes in the streets and waited for someone who needed a message delivered to come by. There were no telephones in those days, so big companies had their own armies of messenger boys.

When telephones were eventually invented and caught on in America, it was thought they'd never take off in Britain. People said there was no need for phones because London was crawling with messenger boys!

A BACK-BREAKING JOB

Children often make good acrobats, because they have shorter limbs and more flexible joints than grown-ups. So some were trained to become **street tumblers** or **circus acrobats**. They were often strapped into strange positions to make them more bendy. One poor boy was stretched so tight, with his head strapped between his knees, that his back broke.

And if you still think working in show business sounds glamorous, what about the children who became known as 'freaks'? If you looked different from other people you could become an exhibit in a 'freak show' for bored crowds to gawp at. This happened to a London lad who weighed over 250 kg and became known as the Fat Boy of Peckham.

JOB SCORE
Acrobat

BOREDOM: maybe
too interesting

DANGER: could bend
yourself out of shape

HARD SLOG:
training takes ages

GLAMOUR:
you'll have an audience

Crossing sweepers made more money on rainy days like this, when the streets were at their muckiest.

BEATING UP A POOR GUY

Nowadays on Bonfire Night you might make a guy out of old clothes and scrunched-up newspapers, but in Victorian London gangs of kids made money by dressing up the littlest lad as a guy and wheeling him round. The problem was that these gangs ended up fighting each other over who should have the best 'patch'. Worse, there were gangs of 'guysmashers', who stole the penny-for-the-guy money and beat up the little one in the guy outfit.

HORSING AROUND WITH HORSE POO

Even before the motorcar, the Victorians had a traffic problem. Their city streets were chock-a-block with carts, buses, and cabs, and there was serious traffic pollution. But rather than petrol fumes, horse-drawn traffic filled the streets with poo. Some kids worked as **crossing sweepers**, cleaning a path through the filth so that posh people could cross the road.

GREAT PILES OF POO

In 1890s London, a hundred tons of horse dung were scraped off the city streets EVERY DAY. That's enough to fill your whole classroom with poo from floor to ceiling. It may have smelt bad, but it meant a lot of work for the orderly boys.

However it was eventually realized that sweeping a lot of muck from one place to another wasn't a very good way of keeping the streets clean. So **orderly boys** were paid to dodge between the horses' hoofs on the busiest streets of the city, shovelling up the manure and tipping it into bins. Not the greatest job in the world, but you did at least get to wear a nice red jumper so people could see you before they ran you over.

JOB SCORE
Crossing sweeper/ orderly boy

💩💩💩
FILTH: horse poo a-plenty

Z Z Z
BOREDOM: stick to your patch all day

☠
DANGER: as long as you know your Green Cross Code

CASH: live off tips

LITTLE SCRUBBERS

JOB SCORE
Stepper

Z Z Z

BOREDOM:
steps all look the same

HARD SLOG:
work till your hands
and knees are red

CASH: very little

GLAMOUR:
nobody notices you

By the nineteenth century, there were several homes run by charities which looked after poor children and orphans. But they put the children to work too. The girls often became **steppers**, going to people's houses and scrubbing doorsteps for a penny each. The people who ran the homes liked to boast about how healthy and happy the little steppers were. Imagine how bad some girls' lives were if it was a step up for them to be scrubbing doorsteps all day long.

THE WEEDY TOWN CHILD

Cities were incredibly unhealthy places. In 1890 Dr Freeman-Williams said that city children were so excitable, neurotic, pale and small, had such bad digestion and were so likely to die young that the whole human race was under threat. He said that if a child's family had lived in London for four generations, then that child would be so weedy it would never survive to adulthood. He was probably wrong; after all, lots of us are alive today!

FLASH KIDS

JOB SCORE
Costermonger

Z Z

BOREDOM:
OK if you like veg

DANGER:
not the riskiest

HARD SLOG:
selling's hard work

CASH: at least
it's your own

A **costermonger** was a person who sold fruit and veg from a stall or barrow in a market. Costermongers started work when they were seven years old, and set up business on their own at fourteen. They were famous for wearing flashy clothes, and had a special code so they could talk in secret in front of their customers and the police. Some of the code was just talking backwards – like 'a top of reeb' for 'a pot of beer' – but it's harder to guess what 'I tumble to your Barrikin' means. (*Answer at bottom of page.*)

* In Costermonger's code 'I tumble to your Barrikin' means 'I understand you'. Although actually I doubt whether many people would have tumbled to their Barrikin.

63

It's very important when you're out nicking things not to get caught. This lad's learning that lesson the hard way.

BAD KIDS

Some children living in the cities turned to **street crime**. It could pay, but it was pretty risky back in the days when just nicking a piece of bread could land you in jail ...

Gangs of **pickpockets**, like the one Oliver joins in *Oliver Twist*, really existed in London. You could learn to be a **'foist'** who picked pockets or a **'nip'** who cut them open. There were even schools for child thieves where the teacher would hang a dummy dressed like a rich person from the ceiling, with alarm bells attached to its pockets. The children had to learn to slip their hands into the pockets without making the bells ring.

JOB SCORE
Pickpocket

BOREDOM:
nice and varied

DANGER: hanging
out with criminals

HARD SLOG:
more tricky than tiring

CASH: good if
you're successful

THIEVING FOR BEGINNERS

1. For picking pockets, choose a crowded place, preferably where people are standing around staring at something like a public hanging.

2. Know your place, and don't upset other young thieves. Remember, skilled pickpockets are at the top of the heap, and they look down on 'nips', who use knives to cut people's purses open. Nips look down on 'pudding-slammers', who lurk outside cook-shops and pinch people's dinners as they come out. Lowest of all are the beggars, who aren't even clever enough to steal for a living.

3. Use your age to fool the grown-ups. Throw your hat into a shop and then crawl in to rob the till. If you get caught, cry and say a bully chucked your hat into the shop, and you were just trying to get it back. Everyone will be nice to you, and you might even get a sweet or a sugared bun!

UP TO YOUR ANKLES IN ...

If you were really poor and desperate you could leave the street, clamber over a fence and try working as a **mudlark**, poking around on the riverbank, among the dead animals, the human sewage and the stinking mud looking for something you could sell, like a handful of copper nails. The work was not only filthy, it could be so cold that some mudlarks deliberately stood in the hot pollution from factory waste pipes to stop their feet from freezing. There was certainly a lot of mud involved in this job, but I can't imagine it was much of a lark.

JOB SCORE
Mudlark

FILTH: in a stinking diseased river

BOREDOM: not likely to find much

HARD SLOG: tough and digusting

CASH: you'll be lucky!

LITTLE BEGGARS

JOB SCORE
Beggar

FILTH: wear your
worst clothes

DANGER: try not to
get beaten up

HARD SLOG:
depressing work

CASH: you won't
see any of it

No one grows up planning to go into **street begging** as a career. It's a horrible job. But some kids were forced to be beggars and didn't even get to keep what they were given. They were hired out to an adult who made them beg for him. In the 1850s for a few shillings a day you could rent a child from its parents to do some begging on your behalf. Some people hired out whole groups of kids, and it cost extra for disabled children or if you kept them out after midnight or if they had to provide their own begging clothes. This was a job where it paid to be pitiful – if you'd had your leg torn off in an accident in the mill or if you had a hunchback from bending over your work making locks or matchboxes, people were more likely to give you money.

But being a kid was no excuse if you got caught begging or stealing. You could still be whipped, put in prison or even hanged. In 1846 two boys from Cambridge who'd been caught stealing fruit were sentenced to be transported to Australia. And a five-year-old girl was put in prison for being a 'vagabond' – which meant being homeless.

A FATE WORSE THAN PRISON

Victorian prisons were meant to be nasty. Birmingham Jail forced prisoners to walk round and round on a treadmill 10,000 times before they were allowed to eat dinner. If you didn't manage it, you'd be tied to a wall and had cold water thrown over you. But some kids' lives were so terrible that prison didn't seem so bad. One boy who was sent to jail couldn't believe his luck. He was amazed that the warders actually gave him socks and shoes to wear, and a proper bed to sleep in. He decided that prison was much nicer than his old job. (He was, you guessed it, a chimney sweep.)

**But the prize for the worst job in the
mean streets has to go to . . .**

The Gong-scourer's Boy!

The **gong-scourer's boy** was probably the smelliest person in human history. He definitely had the worst job in the city streets – or should I say under them. Before there were sewers, not everybody in the city chucked their sewage out of the window into the street – some rich people had toilets that emptied into huge pits of stinking rotten gloop.

Gong-scourers were paid to go into these cesspits and scoop out the mess, which came in two layers: squidged-together solid goo at the bottom, and foul yellowy-brown liquid on top. The adult master scourer was in charge, but he saved the worst bit for his boy assistants. They had to get down in the tightest spaces of the narrowest cesspits and dig out the festering filth.

Gong-scourers had to work at night, because nobody wanted to see (or smell) them doing all this. So if you can't sleep and have no sense of smell, maybe this job is for you.

The powerful stench didn't just make your stomach churn and discourage your friends. It could even kill you. Rotting sewage gives off a gas called hydrogen sulphide, which smells like rotten eggs. If you breathe in too much it can make you keel over and stop breathing. You see, some smells really can be 'silent but deadly'.

JOB SCORE
Gong-scourer

FILTH:
the filthiest job ever?

DANGER:
careful of the gas

HARD SLOG: heavy
work in tight spaces

GLAMOUR:
no glamour whatsoever

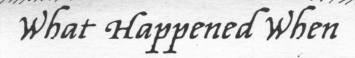

What Happened When

1750 Street lights first introduced in London.
Luckily for the link-boys, they don't catch on right away.

1775 Madame de St-Raymond comes to York to make money from children's teeth.

1800 Over a million people now live in London –
making it the world's biggest city, and a very crowded place.

1824 Twelve-year-old Charles Dickens
sticks labels on to jars – all day, every day …

1832 Cholera kills 20,000 people in Britain.

1837 An eighteen-year-old girl called
Victoria becomes Queen of England.

1838 Dickens's *Oliver Twist* is published.

1858 The 'Great Stink': the Thames gets so disgusting,
MPs run away holding their noses. Mudlarks are pretty much used to it.

1870 Dr Barnardo opens his first home for poor orphan boys.

1886 Karl Benz invents the first
petrol-powered car, signalling the end of horse traffic
in London. Orderly boys are out of a job.

1914–18 Boy Scouts take jobs as
messenger boys in the War Office in London.

2002 There are 60 million people in Britain, and
50 million mobile phones. No need for
messenger boys now.

Service without a Smile

CHAPTER 5

Is life on the streets too tough for you? Would you rather get a job working for rich people who walk on plush carpets and eat loads of mouth-watering food beneath crystal chandeliers?

Before you say, 'Yes! Yes! Please get me away from all this stinking dung! I'll be a servant in a big house instead!' think again. Being a servant involves doing all the stuff rich people think they're too good for.

You'll be working till your knees creak and your thumbs split, and the posh people will totally ignore you. On the very rare occasions when they do decide to speak to you, it'll just be to tell you that you've missed a bit of dirt with your feather duster. You'll certainly see all the fun they have and the amazing places they live in, but you'll never get to join in. Don't worry though ... you won't have time to think about it very much – you'll be too busy.

JOB SCORE
Drawing water

Z Z
BOREDOM:
no fun for kids

DANGER: high risk
of drowning

HARD SLOG: water's
always needed

CASH: little or none

MAKING A SPLASH

Before there was running water from a tap, rich people got water from a **running servant**. Fetching water was a boring, annoying, wet job that no one wanted to do, so usually it got dumped on the youngest and most bully-able servants. This wasn't such a good idea, because getting water from a well is tricky and you could only do it properly if you were strong. Loads of kids were killed trying to lug heavy buckets of water around. Like five-year-old Susan Duncke from Sussex, who went out one spring morning in 1580. She reached into the well with a stone pot, slipped and fell in. By the time anyone could get there to haul her back out, she'd drowned.

IT's JUST WHAT I ALWAYS WANTED

Most servants were given presents by their masters at Christmas. But they were usually even worse than the most embarrassing jumper you've ever got from your nan.

If you were a maid, you might unwrap your parcel to find a length of material – this was for a new dress to wear for work. You might think that doesn't sound so bad, but you had to make the dress yourself or find the money to pay for a tailor.

The rector in a village in Northamptonshire during the First World War must have thought he was pretty generous by comparison: he gave his maid two pig's ears and a pig's tail! It's not quite the same as turkey and all the trimmings but her family ate it anyway.

JOB SCORE
Kennel boy

FILTH:
sleep in the kennels

DANGER:
risk of dogfights

HARD SLOG:
plenty to do

CASH: could have been worse

IN THE DOGHOUSE

You might think that if you were rich you'd never have to be a servant. But that wasn't necessarily true in medieval and Tudor England. If your parents were important, they might get you a job in the household of someone even more rich and powerful than they were.

Lucky me, you might think – unless you were lumbered with a job like being a **kennel boy**. You looked after the lord's hunting dogs and didn't sleep indoors. Instead you went to bed in a draughty hayloft over the kennels.

If the dogs started fighting each other in the middle of the night, you had to get up, go down a ladder, pull the fighting dogs apart, and you wouldn't be able to go back to sleep till you'd managed to quieten them all down and mopped the blood up where they'd bitten you.

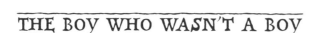

THE BOY WHO WASN'T A BOY

Sunday roast for a Tudor king wasn't just a couple of slices of beef with a few potatoes and peas. He would order up huge lumps of cow, whole porpoises, or a few dozen chickens. These enormous chunks of dead animal were kebabbed in a row on an iron spit. And the person turning the handle was called a **spit-boy**.

Spit-boys worked all morning inside a giant kitchen fireplace, right next to a huge blazing log fire, and they weren't allowed to have a break. There were rules that said that they were not allowed to strip naked when working, even if they were sweating like a pig, and they weren't allowed to pee in the fire either. There must have been an awful lot of sweating, piddling spit-boys, if they had to make special rules to stop them!

Some people think that spit-boys wouldn't really have been boys, but adult men who were called 'boys' as a kind of insult because their job was so lowly. But no one really knows. What do you think – how old do you think the spit-boy looks in this picture?

JOB SCORE
Spit-boy

FILTH: OK if you don't wee in the fire

BOREDOM: keep that handle turning

HARD SLOG: it's heavy and your skin burns

GLAMOUR: no seat at dinner for you

SLAVES TO FASHION

JOB SCORE
Black pageboy

FILTH:
try to stay clean

ZZZ

BOREDOM:
not much to do

CASH:
slaves don't get paid

★ ★

GLAMOUR: you're
the height of fashion

*What do you think
he really thinks of
his mistress?*

How would you fancy spending your life looking smart and serving your mistress hot chocolate? A **black pageboy** was thought a very trendy accessory in the seventeenth century. A fashionable lady would often take a little well-dressed black boy around with her, and have her portrait painted with him to show off how rich she was. These were designed to make the lady's skin seem whiter, because in those days posh people wanted to look as if they'd never been outdoors or done any exercise in their lives.

It doesn't sound like the job would have been too hard. But the pages were mostly slaves, brought over in misery from Africa or the Caribbean. Imagine how homesick they must have been. They were often advertised for sale in the newspapers. One ad said:

'To be sold, a negro boy aged eleven years. Enquire at the Virginia Coffee House in Threadneedle Street ... his price is £25.'

Not that he'd see any of the cash, of course.

75

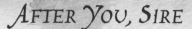

After You, Sire

A pageboy is a little lad in a shiny waistcoat at a wedding who gets bored and fidgets during the ceremony. But if you were a boy page to a great lord in the seventeenth century, you had a much more serious job. Not only did you have to wait on him hand and foot, but if there was a war you'd have to go into battle with him.

When King Charles I's son James went into battle with his dad he was only nine.

It was good training for him to stand and watch as his dad's soldiers charged the enemy and got impaled on the long pikes they held. With dying horses crushing their screaming riders, and the bangs and smell of gunpowder from muskets, the battle wasn't something James was going to forget in a hurry.

EASY, TIGER

If you were a particularly short lad and quite smart-looking, you might get a job as a **tiger**. It wasn't too hard: you stood on the back of a carriage while your master was driving, and then got off and held the horse's head when he wanted to get out. But the tiger who worked for the prime minister Lord Salisbury had a sillier and tougher job. His Lordship liked riding his tricycle around the grounds of his house, and made his tiger stand on the back as if it was a carriage. When they got to the bottom of a slope, the tiger had to jump off and push the fat old politician uphill. He must have felt a real plonker!

JOB SCORE
Tiger

FILTH: look smart at all times

BOREDOM: all you do is look smart

HARD SLOG: get a lift everywhere

GLAMOUR: ride behind the poshest coaches

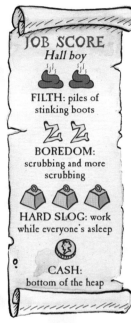
STINKY BOOTS

In some big Edwardian country houses, there were over thirty servants – and right at the bottom of the ladder was the **hall boy**. These were local lads, and could be as young as eight. They would work from 6 a.m. to 10 p.m., or longer if the family were giving a late-night dinner or party. It must have been a nightmare, cleaning the boots and shoes of the entire household, including any visitors, plus all the servants. If the guests had come for a shooting party, their boots would have been caked in mud, but they'd still have to be polished till they shone.

The boots and shoes couldn't be collected until after their wearers had staggered off to bed, however late it might be, and they had to be spick and span before breakfast at eight the next morning. So the poor old hall boys can't have got much sleep!

77

CAUGHT RED-HANDED

People living in big houses had big dinners. And big dinners created a mountain of washing up. According to one Edwardian butler, ten people used 324 items of silver, glass and china during a single meal, not to mention all the saucepans and knives in the kitchen. Imagine having to scrub away at that lot!

Scullery maids had to learn the right way to wash all the different bits and pieces to get them really clean. For instance, they had to dip the glasses in hot water and then in cold water with a bit of soda in it. The hot water had to be almost boiling, and the soda made their skin dry and cracked. You could always tell a scullery maid by her red scabby hands.

JOB SCORE
Scullery maid

FILTH:
endless greasy pans

BOREDOM:
not much variety

DANGER: too dull
to be dangerous

HARD SLOG:
real drudgery

SNUFFING IT

Question: How many children does it take to change a lightbulb?
Answer: Not as many as it took before lightbulbs were invented.

Lightbulbs need changing only every few months – lamps and candles had to be checked, changed and cleaned every single day. **Lamp-boys** in big Victorian country houses might have to go round hundreds of oil lamps cleaning them, filling them with oil and trimming their wicks.

The Marquis of Bath's **candle-boy** used to have to go round his chapel every morning after the service, snuffing out the candles, breaking off the dribbly bits of wax and remoulding the candle tops with his fingers so they were neat and pointy again. Fine if there

JOB SCORE
Lamp-boy

FILTH: fairly mucky

BOREDOM:
at least you go all
round the house

HARD SLOG:
a whole lot of lamps

CASH:
won't get you rich

were just a couple of candles on the altar — but in the marquis's chapel there were 140 of them. Not that this was the full extent of his candle-boy's work. He also had to sort out all 400 lamps in the rest of the house. He must have ended up stinking of oil, covered in bits of wax, and was probably a bit of a fire hazard himself.

Oi, You

Some rich people couldn't be bothered to remember all their servants' names, so they gave them new ones. Maybe you were Clara, but you'd be called Ann because the parlourmaids in that house were always called Ann. That way, the family could get rid of you and hire a new maid and hardly notice the difference.

Or your real name might be Tom, but if the boy of the family was also called Tom you might become Arthur instead.

MAID THE TEA, MAID THE BED, MAID THE ...

There were lots of different kinds of **maids** in nineteenth-century houses: housemaids, kitchen maids, parlourmaids, scullery maids, nursery maids ... Many were young girls fresh from the countryside. Employers often thought it was a good idea to hire girls from a long way away because they wouldn't have any friends to distract them while they were working. A maid could ask to go out sometimes to meet new friends, but permission was often refused, and she definitely wasn't allowed to have boyfriends.

Maids usually shared a room in an unheated, damp attic above their masters' lovely clean, comfortable quarters. Some employers even put glass windows in their maids' bedroom doors so they could check they weren't wasting candles by reading in bed. If you were a maid, you had to follow rules like these:

· You must stay out of sight of the family.
If you're working upstairs and you hear someone coming, disappear.
Good maids should be invisible.

· Don't walk in the garden unless you're sure everyone in the family's out.

· No singing, whistling or talking where the family can hear you.

- Don't speak until you're spoken to and use as few words as you can when you answer.

- Stand aside when a lady or gentleman passes in the corridor.

- Don't talk to other servants when the family are present.

- Call the family 'ma'am', 'miss' or 'sir'.

- Don't touch the family. If you have to pass them something, put it on a silver tray first.

- If you are out walking with a lady or gentleman, stay a few paces behind them.

- If you're in the room when the family are having a conversation, pretend you're not listening. If someone tells a joke, keep a straight face and act like part of the furniture.

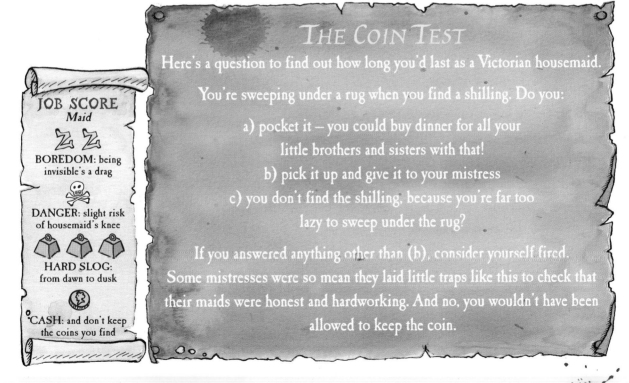

JOB SCORE
Maid

Z Z

BOREDOM: being invisible's a drag

DANGER: slight risk of housemaid's knee

HARD SLOG: from dawn to dusk

CASH: and don't keep the coins you find

THE COIN TEST

Here's a question to find out how long you'd last as a Victorian housemaid.

You're sweeping under a rug when you find a shilling. Do you:

a) pocket it – you could buy dinner for all your little brothers and sisters with that!

b) pick it up and give it to your mistress

c) you don't find the shilling, because you're far too lazy to sweep under the rug?

If you answered anything other than (b), consider yourself fired. Some mistresses were so mean they laid little traps like this to check that their maids were honest and hardworking. And no, you wouldn't have been allowed to keep the coin.

But the worst thing was the work itself. Even dusting was exhausting in a big old house full of expensive ornaments, with the air polluted by smoke and dust from the coal fires.

It would be a long time before everyone had a Hoover or a Dyson. To clean the dust out of rugs, maids had to get down on their knees, scatter dried tea leaves to collect the dust and stop the rug smelling, and then sweep the tea up again. And to polish the fire grates and the cooking ranges they had to mix up their own 'blacking' polish from ivory black, treacle, oil, beer and sulphuric acid. You could buy this stuff ready-made, but what was the point when there was a poor girl who could make it at home?

FOUR HOURS' SLEEP

In the early nineteenth century Mrs Wollaston of Clapham put an advert in the paper for a new maid. On Mondays this maid would have to get up at 1 a.m. and do the laundry until 5 or 6 a.m., then clean the house till 11 a.m., before going back to the laundry until 9 p.m. Getting up at 6 a.m. the rest of the week must have felt like a long lie-in.

FLAT NEWS

I hate it when my newspaper's all crumpled. It can ruin my whole day. Some Victorian gentlemen felt so strongly about this that they got their maids to iron their copy of *The Times* each morning, and even had them sew the pages together so they didn't fall apart when they were reading it. Maybe they thought their servants weren't busy enough ...

6·30 a.m.
OPEN CURTAINS AND WINDOWS IN NURSERY, SHAKE RUG OUTSIDE, CLEAN GRATE, LIGHT FIRE, PUT OUT COAL BUCKETS. WASH FLOOR, DUST FURNITURE AND LAY TABLE FOR NURSERY BREAKFAST. CLEAN CHILDREN'S SHOES. CLEAN THE MORNING ROOM.

8·00 a.m.
TAKE UP NURSERY BREAKFAST. HAVE YOUR OWN BREAKFAST.

8·35 a.m.
AIR THE BEDS IN THE NURSERY, YOUR OWN ROOM AND THE FRONT BEDROOM. EMPTY HOT WATER BOTTLES, FOLD NIGHT CLOTHES AND TIDY ROOM. CLEAR NURSERY TABLE. HELP NURSE CARRY UP BABY'S BATH. MAKE BEDS, EMPTY AND WASH OUT THE CHAMBER-POTS. SWEEP BEDROOM FLOORS. BRUSH LANDING AND STAIR CARPETS, DUST FURNITURE AND DOORS.

10·15 a.m.
WASH DINING ROOM BREAKFAST DISHES AND NURSERY DISHES.

10·30 a.m.
CLEAN HALL BRASSES. CLEAN SERVANTS HALL, SWEEP CELLAR STEPS AND OUTSIDE LAVATORY.

12·15 p.m.
CLEAN BATHROOM AND LAVATORY. LAY TABLE FOR NURSERY LUNCH.

1·00 p.m.
TAKE UP NURSERY LUNCH AND HAVE YOUR OWN. WASH UP IN SCULLERY. LAY OUT NURSERY TEA.

2·30 p.m.
TAKE BABY FOR A WALK,

PUSHING THE SECOND PRAM.

4·15 p.m.
LAY TEA IN SERVANTS' HALL. CLEAR AWAY AND WASH UP.

5·00 p.m.
BRING DOWN NURSERY TEA THINGS, WASH AND TAKE BACK.

6·00 p.m.
SEWING AND MENDING FOR MISTRESS.

7·30 p.m.
LAY TABLE FOR SUPPER IN SERVANTS' HALL

7·45 p.m.
HELP WAIT ON TABLE WITH PARLOURMAID. DURING DINNER, GO UPSTAIRS AND TURN DOWN BEDS. WASH UP IN PANTRY.

10·00 p.m.
BED!

But the prize for the very worst job in someone else's house has to go to . . .

The Maid-of-all-work!

Not everyone could afford lots of housemaids, parlourmaids, nursery maids and so on. Families who hadn't got enough money to surround themselves with servants often had to make do with just one – and she was known as a **maid-of-all-work**. She had to do all the things the housemaid on the previous page did, but that was just the start. She also did all the cooking, cleaned the boots, ran errands and answered the door.

Maids-of-all-work were usually teenagers, often as young as thirteen years old, because no one with any experience would have taken such a rotten job.

But the saddest thing about their lives must have been the loneliness. Unlike other maids, they were all on their own. Imagine what it must have been like, stuck in the kitchen all by yourself for hours, with only the ticking clock for company. Other servants might have had a pretty rotten time, but no one could have had quite as miserable a life as a maid-of-all-work. Even the kennel boy had his dogs to talk to.

What Happened When

1397 King Richard II throws a mammoth feast, giving his spit-boys a severe case of heatstroke.

1642 Battle of Edge Hill. Nine-year-old James, Duke of York, dodges cannonballs as his dad's side wins the battle … just.

1802 A Mr Phair writes a guide on how to install bells all round your house so you can call your servants. The servants aren't impressed: they now get to spend half their time running up and down stairs whenever a bell rings.

1807 Slavery is abolished in England. Now nobody wants to have a little well-dressed black boy following them everywhere. It wouldn't be cool any more. It would make them look like an old-fashioned slave-owner!

1886 A rich American called Josephine Cochran invents the dishwasher — not to make life easier for her servants, but because she thinks they're lousy at washing-up. But dishwashers don't become popular until the 1950s, by which time more people can afford them.

1901 Hubert Cecil Booth invents the vacuum cleaner — before that, you had to sweep up the dust with tea leaves, a brush and a dustpan.

1914 The First World War begins. While the men are away, girls take over their jobs in factories.

1918 The girls in the factories don't want to go back to being servants. People in posh houses have to buy vacuum cleaners instead.

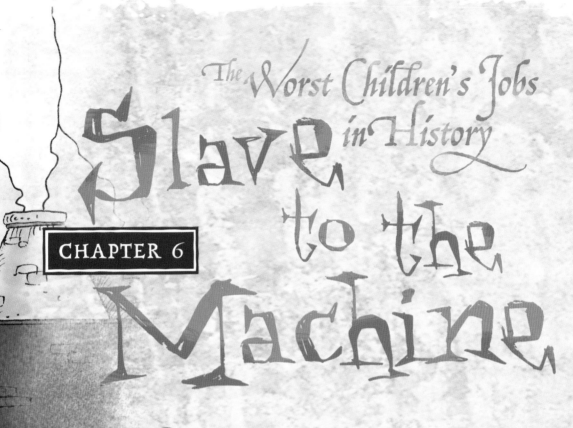

The Worst Children's Jobs in History

CHAPTER 6

Slave to the Machine

OK, so it was grim to scrub floors, climb chimneys or work aboard a fishing boat on a stormy sea, but now we're going to enter a whole new dimension of working misery.

The jobs that came out of the Industrial Revolution, when Britain became the richest nation in the world, shocked the whole nation. Clever men in tall hats and daft beards invented new machines that made complicated work so easy a child could do it – and tens of thousands of them did.

TROUBLE AT T'MILL

Cotton mills could be very scary places. Huge machines made of wood and metal clattered, rattled, swished, banged, whirred, thudded and clunked away non-stop. They may have made Britain rich. But for the kids who worked in them, they were hellish prisons where you could easily go deaf or lose a hand.

The spinning mule was a machine that spun cotton thread much faster than a spinning wheel could. If you were a **piecer**, your job was to stick any broken pieces of cotton together while the mule was moving. In order to do this you had to spit on the ends and then twist them backwards and forwards, which made your fingers bleed.

JOB SCORE
Piecer

FILTH: clouds
of cotton

ZZZ
BOREDOM:
so dull it hurts

DANGER:
moderate for a factory

HARD SLOG:
work till you drop

And you weren't allowed to sit down while you were doing it. The machine moved right across the room and back as it wound thread on to bobbins, and you had to walk alongside it without stopping. By the end of the day you'd have walked about twenty miles, and you'd be pretty sweaty, because mill owners liked to heat the mills to a steamy 27°C to stop the cotton from breaking.

Some of the piecers were as young as six. When John Lombe began work in 1730, he was so short he couldn't reach his machine. The other workers had to tie big wooden blocks to his feet so that he could get on with the job.

88

The girl in this picture is a piecer, and the boy scrabbling around under the machine is a scavenger. Do these look like good jobs? I don't think so.

JOB SCORE
Scavenger

FILTH:
dusty, filthy floors

DANGER: risky
machinery everywhere

HARD SLOG:
follow that machine

CASH:
insultingly little

While the mule was spinning and the piecer was piecing, bits of cotton fluff drifted under the machines. They had to be cleaned away because they could cause a fire. The easiest way to get rid of them was for a small child to crawl under the machine with a brush. This had to be done while the machine was working, because if it ever stopped it lost the boss money.

The children who did this, usually the youngest at the mill, were called **scavengers** and they risked getting their heads, arms, legs, hands and toes crushed by the moving machinery. It was especially dangerous when they were hungry or tired. (Remember, they started work at 5.30 in the morning.)

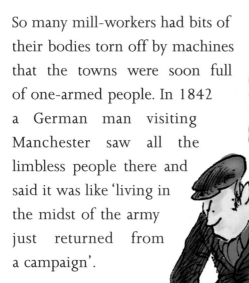

So many mill-workers had bits of their bodies torn off by machines that the towns were soon full of one-armed people. In 1842 a German man visiting Manchester saw all the limbless people there and said it was like 'living in the midst of the army just returned from a campaign'.

TIMETABLE
for cotton mill-workers in 1830

5.30 a.m. Start work.

8.30 a.m. Ten-minute break to eat your breakfast.

1.00 p.m. Thirty-minute break to go home for dinner.

5.30 p.m. Eat your tea at your machine.

8.00 p.m. Go home, if you're not doing overtime that day.

YUM, YUM ... COTTON WOOL!

The air in a cotton mill was permanently full of white fluff. If you left your lunch lying around, you'd have to dust it off before you ate it or it would be like chewing cotton wool.

The fluff got in your nose, in your eyes and, worst of all, into your lungs. Cotton workers usually had bad asthma. But when factories started putting fans in to clear the air, the workers didn't like it. They said they were so used to swallowing bits of fluffy cotton that they got hungry without it!

USING YOUR HEAD

In brick factories children had to carry great lumps of cold, wet clay. In 1870 the writer George Smith met a nine-year-old girl in one of these factories who walked twelve and a half miles back and forth every day, fetching clay to dump on the brickmaker's bench. She carried it on her head, and each load weighed 20 kg. She must have had a really strong neck to do that!

If you want to know what 20 kg feels like, you'll need to pile forty tins of baked beans on to your head. But I shouldn't bother unless you really like beans. In York there were reports that children in the brickyards were drinking booze with the adult workers and getting drunk. This can't have made balancing the clay very easy, can it?

A picture from George Smith's book about the brickyards. These kids must have had permanent headaches.

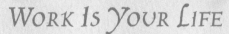

WORK IS YOUR LIFE

All children in factories worked ridiculously long hours. Some of them were so-called 'apprentices', who slept in dormitories at the factory, but even if they lived with their parents they would hardly ever see them.

'It is almost the general system for the little children in these manufacturing villages to know nothing of their parents at all excepting that in the morning very early, at 5 o'clock, very often before 4, they are awakened by a human being that they are told is their father, and are pulled out of bed (I have heard many a score of them give account of it) when they are almost asleep, and lesser children are absolutely carried on the backs of the older children asleep to the mill, and they see no more of their parents, generally speaking, till they go home at night, and are sent to bed.'

– A factory inspector

DEADLY JUMPERS

Cotton made you cough, but wool weavers had an even bigger problem. The wool could give them a disease called anthrax. One day they'd be short of breath and have a sore throat. Then they'd get tired, shivery and start throwing up. They'd have to spend the next day in bed, and on day three they'd probably be dead. If they didn't die they got terrible skin blisters, paralysed fingers and fevers that kept coming back.

92

JOB SCORE
Jigger-turner

FILTH: the least
of your worries

BOREDOM:
and an aching arm

HARD SLOG:
constant effort

GLAMOUR: even
the job title's silly

Pottery's a hobby, right? It's how you make those rubbish wobbly pots to give your mum on Mother's Day. Well, in the nineteenth century, potteries were big business. Stoke-on-Trent was full of them – big factories churning out fancy teacups, dinner plates and vases. They were hot, dusty, dangerous places, full of poisonous clay-dust and lead glaze. And they were packed with jobs for children.

The **jigger-turners** rotated a handle all day to make the potter's wheel go round. The little girls who did this must have felt as though their arms were about to drop off. It was the kind of job that could have been done just as well by a machine. But no one bothered, because children were cheaper.

A jigger-turner turning his jigger in Stoke-on-Trent.

Some small boys had the job of making handles for teacups. First, they put a piece of clay in between two halves of a mould. Then they bashed the mould together by squashing it with their chest. In 1841 a potteries inspector warned that the way the boys bounced down on the moulds was highly dangerous and would flatten their chests and squish their innards out of shape.

The **mould-runner** probably had the worst job in the potteries. He carried freshly made plate moulds filled with heavy clay back and forth from the unheated workshop to the hot drying room. These rooms were heated to over 50°C, so it was a bit like running in and out of a sauna all day. The inspector of the potteries calculated that mould-runners had to run over seven miles each day. And they really did have to run, because it took less time to mould each plate than to carry it to the kiln. If he was late getting back, he'd get walloped by the man filling the moulds.

JOB SCORE
Mould-runner

💤💤
BOREDOM:
fairly repetitive

☠☠
DANGER: some
poisonous pottery dust

HARD SLOG:
run like the wind

CASH: still no wealth

The girl in this picture may look as though she's biting her lip – but in fact half her jaw has been eaten away.

JOB SCORE
Match-making

FILTH:
stinking sulphur

DANGER:
could lose your jaw

HARD SLOG: as bad
as other factories

CASH: very lowly

JOB SCORE
Cutlery grinding

FILTH: tiny bits of
metal everywhere

BOREDOM:
averagely boring

HARD SLOG: famous
for being hard work

DANGER: could get
metal in your eye

MEETING YOUR MATCH

One of the most horrible diseases you could get from working in a factory was the dreaded 'phossy jaw'. If you were young girl in a match factory in East London, you really didn't want to get a rotten tooth, because it could be attacked by the fumes from the phosphorous in which you dipped the matches. You could well end up with your whole jawbone eaten away, and your empty cheek black and oozing foul-smelling green gunk. It was agony, and it happened to girls as young as eleven.

NOSE TO THE GRINDSTONE

Sheffield in the nineteenth century was full of cutlery factories. And these factories were full of dust. Boys of nine and up spent their days leaning over a grinding wheel, shaping steel knives and forks. Tiny particles of stone dust flew off the wheel and into the boys' lungs, which caused a disease called silicosis. It made them very wheezy, with a painful chest and a hacking cough, and they lost a lot of weight very quickly. Putting your nose to the grindstone might be good for getting things done, but it wasn't very healthy if you were a **boy cutler**.

DEATH METAL

Grease boy, **rubber**, **puller-up**, **hooker-on** and **pickle-and-scale boy** sound like insults, but actually they are all jobs that used to be done by children in metalworks. These kids worked twelve-hour shifts in sweltering heat, breathing in sulphurous fumes which smelt of rotten eggs and stunted their growth. In copper works in Wales, some boys worked 24-hour shifts shovelling coal into the furnaces. This needed to be done every two hours, so when they got the chance to have a quick nap it wasn't for very long.

JOB SCORE
Metalworks boy

FILTH: hot and sweaty

BOREDOM:
better than some

DANGER:
terrible accidents

HARD SLOG:
lots of heavy weights

There were several ways of getting killed or injured in a metalworks. There was molten metal all over the place, which gave you a terrible burn if it got on your skin. But young Thomas George had an even worse experience. He slipped and fell while working in an iron-rolling mill, and his left arm got caught between the rollers. His mates quickly grabbed him, turned off the machine and managed to save his life, but he lost all of his arm except for a short stump.

GOING UNDERGROUND

Are you ever scared of the dark? If so, this next job would have been your personal worst-job hell. Lots of factories needed coal for power, and coal had always come from far underground, down dark, damp, dangerous tunnels. But thanks to new technology, mines could now be dug even deeper, with narrow tunnels running literally miles underground. And dotted all through these ant-farm-like tunnels were children, who could fit into the tightest space and would work for hardly any money.

The jobs they did down there were as bad as in the factories, with the added downside that those who worked day shifts saw sunlight only once a week.

HURRYING ALONG

A **hurrier** was a boy or girl who worked on their hands and knees in the deepest tunnels, dragging cartloads of coal behind them on a chain attached to their belt. Scabby knees were the least of the hurrier's worries – you'd have hardly noticed them when your muscles were screaming and you'd got a crippling backache.

The tunnels were often dripping wet, so the children would spend all day in sopping wet clothes. Ponies were sometimes used for this job, but ponies are bigger than children. To make room for them, money had to be spent on wider tunnels, and the pit owners were often too stingy to do this. In fact, most of them only started using ponies when the government banned child labour.

Not all children down the mines pulled coal carts, some pushed them! By the time she was seventeen, Patience Kershaw had worn a bald patch on her head from pushing so many carts uphill. And in Scotland, girls carried the coal up ladders and along passageways in baskets on their backs.

JOB SCORE
Hurrier

FILTH: covered in coal dust

BOREDOM: not much to look at

DANGER: could get trapped underground

HARD SLOG: real donkey-work

Kids pushing and pulling a huge pile of coal to the mine shaft. It can't have helped that the tunnel sloped uphill.

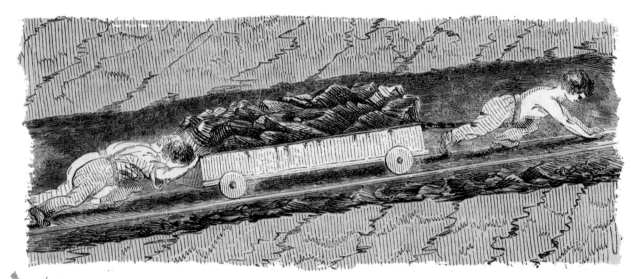

98

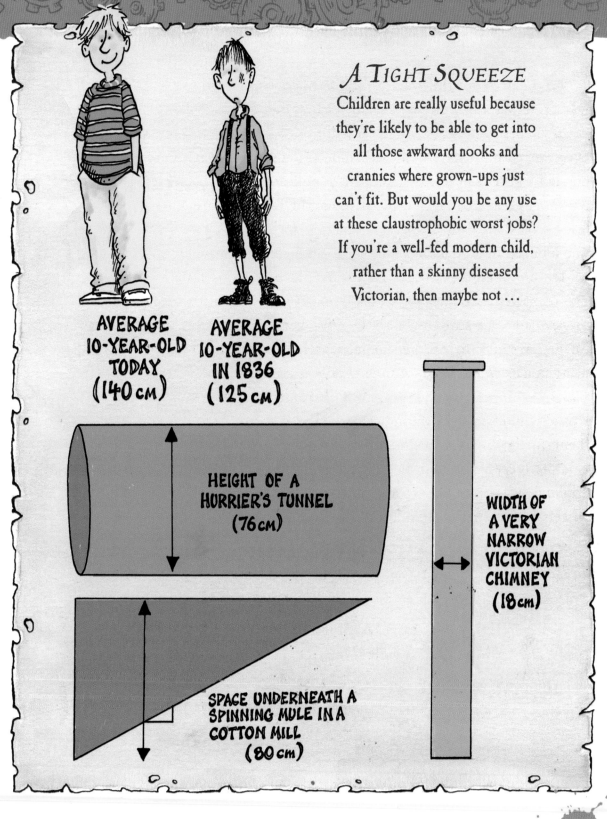

A TIGHT SQUEEZE

Children are really useful because they're likely to be able to get into all those awkward nooks and crannies where grown-ups just can't fit. But would you be any use at these claustrophobic worst jobs? If you're a well-fed modern child, rather than a skinny diseased Victorian, then maybe not ...

AVERAGE 10-YEAR-OLD TODAY (140 cm)

AVERAGE 10-YEAR-OLD IN 1836 (125 cm)

HEIGHT OF A HURRIER'S TUNNEL (76 cm)

WIDTH OF A VERY NARROW VICTORIAN CHIMNEY (18 cm)

SPACE UNDERNEATH A SPINNING MULE IN A COTTON MILL (80 cm)

And the prize for the loneliest job in history has to go to ...

The Trapper

The **trapper** must have been the saddest, loneliest kid in history. Boys and girls as young as six opened 'trap-doors' in the tunnels whenever a cart needed to come past. For the rest of the time, they just sat on their own in the dark, waiting for the next cart. They weren't even allowed a candle, because candles cost money.

They couldn't leave their post for a minute just in case a door needed opening. It must have been mind-numbingly boring and pretty frightening. You'd lose all sense of time sitting alone all day in the dark, wouldn't you? And I bet after a few hours you'd start hearing things!

A trapper who's probably quite excited to see a cart. After all, it does have a light on the front!

SHUT YOUR TRAP

The trapper's job was vitally important for the safety of all the miners. He had to keep his door shut whenever possible to stop dangerous gases from building up. In Burdon Main Colliery in 1835, ten-year-old trapper Joseph Arkley might have got bored and nodded off, or maybe he just wandered away from his door, letting it stand open for a few minutes.

Unfortunately we don't know exactly what happened because that's when his boss came round with a candle, which set light to the gas. The explosion ripped through the tunnel and killed eleven people, including young Joseph.

What Happened When

1730   John Lombe starts work at a cotton mill – even though he's too short to reach the machines.

1771   Ex-lather-boy Richard Arkwright opens the first water-powered spinning mill on the River Derwent at Cromford, Derbyshire.

1819   The Factory Act stops children from working in factories or cotton mills before their ninth birthday. But some parents need the cash so much, they lie about their children's ages.

1823   The first cutlery factory opens in Sheffield. More kids can now get sick with silicosis, and all under the same roof – that's progress!

1830   In Manchester, Richard Roberts designs a mule for spinning cotton that moves automatically. This machine opens up some great worst jobs for piecers and scavengers.

1842   The government bans boys under ten from going underground in mines, and women and girls aren't allowed to work underground at all.

1864   The government says all factories have to be clean and well ventilated, but girls in cotton mills complain about the lack of fluff to swallow. There's no pleasing some people, is there?

1871   George Smith publishes a pamphlet called *The Cry of The Children from the Brickyards of England.* I wonder if the cry was, 'Ouch, my flipping neck's sore.'

1888   At the Bryant and May match factory in East London, match girls organize a strike to complain about their working conditions. Little things are bothering them, like the fines they have to pay for dropping matches or going to the toilet, and the way their faces keep falling to bits. The company stopped the fines – but continued using the risky phosphorus till 1901.

P.S.

Reading about some of the jobs in this book might have made you feel sick. But the odd thing is that the children who did them would have been so used to them that they might not have thought their work was bad at all. If there was no such thing as Ariel Meadow Fresh to help you get your whites whiter, then you'd probably be only too glad to use a bit of wee mixed with water.

I wonder what people in 500 years' time will think of your life. They'll probably be horrified.

'Were their streets really full of stinking petrol-driven cars?' they may say. 'How on earth did they breathe?'

'Did they really eat dead animals? And wasn't it cruel, making them stay in school for six hours every day?'

'And I can't believe they actually had to read books. Wasn't life horrible in those days!'

INDEX

If you want to find out more about the foul and terrifying jobs your great-great-great-granny might have done, try a day out at some of these places.

Washerboys

- Killhope – North of England Lead Mining Museum, Upper Weardale, County Durham www.durham.gov.uk/killhope

Mill damsels

- Shugborough, Staffordshire www.shugborough.net

Servants

- Lanhydrock, Bodmin, Cornwall – kitchen, larder, servants' quarters www.nationaltrust.org.uk/hbcache/property5.htm

Spit-boys and kennel boys

- Hampton Court, East Molesey, Surrey www.hrp.org.uk/webcode/hampton_home.asp

Trappers and hurriers

- Big Pit – National Mining Museum of Wales, Blaenafon, Torfaen www.nmgw.ac.uk/www.php/bigpit/
- National Coal Mining Museum for England, Overton, Wakefield www.ncm.org.uk/

Piecers and scavengers

- Quarry Bank Mill, Wilmslow, Cheshire www.quarrybankmill.org.uk/

Jigger-turners and mould-runners

- Gladstone Potteries, Stoke-on-Trent www2002.stoke.gov.uk/museums/gpm_main.html

Workhouses and farming

- Gressenhall, Dereham, Norfolk www.museums.norfolk.gov.uk/default.asp?Document=200.50

Nail-making

- Black Country Living Museum, Dudley, West Midlands www.bclm.co.uk

General/Daily life

- Ironbridge, Coalbrookdale, Shropshire – see iron-working and look round a reconstructed Victorian town. Also pop in to Coalport China Museum, to see how the jigger-turners and mould-runners worked www.ironbridge.co.uk
- North of England Open Air Museum, Beamish, County Durham – mining town of the early 1900s www.beamish.org.uk
- Museum of Childhood, Bethnal Green, London – has an ongoing exhibition of children at work www.vam.ac.uk/vastatic/nmc/
- Weald and Downland Open Air Museum, Chichester, West Sussex – Tudor farm, medieval cottage www.wealddown.co.uk
- Museum of Welsh Life, St Fagans, Cardiff www.nmgw.ac.uk/www.php/mwl/